Bloods, Wigs and Tears

Michelle Canny

ISBN: 9798525509290

Hello Mr Magpie,
how's your wife and kids?

Sat 20th June 2015

I was in the bath when I felt it. It was hard and stretched across the top half of my left breast. My heart lurched, and I felt it again just to make sure I wasn't mistaken. It was definitely there, a hard repulsive lump, and I was immediately petrified. That would be the first and the last time I would ever touch it.

We'd had a really lovely day at Culdaff beach. I had flown over to Ireland with my children, Ethan and Orla, to try and cheer up my childhood friend, Julie who was going through a marriage break up and also the sudden, unexpected loss of her father. Julie was a mate who'd moved to Donegal many years earlier. My husband and I had bought a house in the same county as it was where my husband was from, and we regularly used it as our holiday home. My sister Fiona, who lives in Derry, was down with her two kids, Gracie Lee and Odhran, and Julie was down with her son, Jack.

The sun had shone, and the kids had built sandcastles. I hadn't been very organised and took a bucket but no spade. The kids didn't care and dug holes with their bare hands. We laughed as Fiona aimed the camera to try and obtain the 'perfect photograph' and had the kids jumping in the air or posing on the sandbank. Julie and I were happy for Fiona to take charge, as we were feeling slightly hungover from the night before in Carndonagh.

I got out of the bath and wrapped myself in my husband Liam's grey dressing gown, then went into my bedroom and tried to understand what I had just felt. Orla, my ten-year-old daughter, stared straight at me and asked, 'Are you okay, Mum?' I realised that she was so perfectly in tune with me that I needed to forget temporarily about it. I nodded and mumbled, 'Everything is fine.'

Fiona was in the kitchen having pre-outing drinks whilst Julie showered. She also looked at me and asked, 'Are you okay?'

I responded with a simple 'yes', pulled back the ring pull on my Koppenburg and took a large mouthful.

We were going out that night, so what was the point of pulling the rug from under them? It was the weekend, and I was in Ireland; nothing was going to make any difference telling them now or another day. Liam texted and I put off telling him, too; I would tell him on my return to Luton the next day.

We had a great night out in Gleneely and then heading to Carndonagh. Fiona was high on life and drunk on vodka, and she made us laugh our heads off with her crazy dancing. But I still couldn't shift the black cloud looming above my head, and I was more than happy to go home when Fiona suggested it.

When I woke up the next morning, I made my mind up that I didn't want to let Liam know quite yet. I wanted another day of being me and not a victim, another day of not being treated any differently. Also, Julie was going through a really tough time, so throwing my problem into the mix wasn't even a thought.

We tidied the house, embraced, and my children and I headed to Belfast airport for our flight to the UK. Liam was there to meet us, and we went to our local pub and restaurant, O'Sheas, where we had a gorgeous meal and the kids told Liam about their brilliant holiday.

Liam was a bit preoccupied; he'd recently lost a wonderful Polish employee who had been killed in Poland a few weeks previously, and his brother was falling to bits. It was definitely not the day to tell my husband what I'd found.

On Monday morning, I made my way to the vets where I work as a veterinary nurse. I decided to ring the doctor to make an emergency appointment for that day. Everyone in Luton must have been trying too, because the phone rang and rang for about fifteen minutes.

Eventually I got through. I went downstairs into the cellar so nobody could hear what I was about to say. Even saying the words out loud to the receptionist made me feel physically sick; suddenly it all seemed so real, and I could feel myself welling up.

I explained the urgency to the receptionist. She was very sympathetic and made an appointment with a female doctor at a branch surgery for 3.45pm. I muddled through the day at work and was so relieved when it was finally 1.30pm and I could leave. I decided to tell Liam as he would have to do one of the school pickups. When I went to his workplace, his brother and my baby niece, Isla-rose, were there. I nursed Isla-rose and made idle chit- chat, willing my brother-in-law to go so I could talk to my husband.

When they finally left, I sat in Liam's office staring at the computer screen and whispered in a small voice that I had to go to the doctor. Liam asked why. I didn't take my eyes from the computer screen as I told him that I'd found a lump in my breast and wanted to get it checked out.

Liam took a large intake of breath, but he didn't speak for what seemed like several minutes.

Then he asked me, 'What do you mean, a lump? When? How? Where?'

I can't remember what I said because, as soon as I let my eyes leave the computer screen and saw his crestfallen face, I broke down. I slipped my sunglasses over my eyes and sobbed as he hugged me tight.

I made my way to the dreaded appointment. This was going to be the game changer. Maybe I hadn't felt the lump at all; maybe it was just something that had already dispersed. Maybe the doctor would pat me on the back, tell me it was all a big mistake and send me on my way back to my normal life. Unfortunately, that was not the case.

'Michelle Canny,' came the call, and I followed the doctor into the consulting room. I sat down and explained that I'd only found the lump forty-eight hours earlier and how worried I was.

'When was your last period?' she asked me.

I couldn't remember. 'Possibly a few weeks ago, I'm not sure.'

'It is disgusting that, as a woman, you don't keep a log,' she barked back at me with contempt in her voice.

She asked me to lie on the bed and at the same time asked why, as a Farley Hill patient, I was being seen at this surgery. I explained that the receptionist had booked me an appointment with the first available female doctor, which happened to be at this branch. She huffed and said in a clipped voice that this was happening far too often.

I stood there in disbelief; had she not heard me? Had she not seen how petrified I was? How could someone be so cold and heartless? I wanted to leave that consulting room door and forget all about it. Where the feck was her bedside manner?

I stripped off my top half and lay on the bed. The doctor continued to complain; evidently the last person who'd used her room had not replaced the paper sheet on the bed. She finally began to examine me.

As she was removing her latex gloves, she informed me in a very matter-of-fact voice that there was a lump of approximately four inches across the top of my left breast. Four inches? Holy fuck –that was not good. Jesus Christ above!

She explained that, due to its sudden appearance, she would refer me and I would be seen within two weeks. I broke down, but she simply responded that it might be a cyst and I should try not to worry.

In a panic I asked, 'What if I go private?'

She didn't lift her eyes from the computer monitor as she replied that it would be the same timeframe.

I walked out of the room with my sunglasses on so that the people in the waiting room couldn't see the tears streaming down my face. I made my way outside and, in the sanctuary of my car, I howled like a new-born baby.

I rang Liam. He had the two kids in the car as he was on his way back from picking up Ethan from school. I muttered, 'Do you want to go to the park and walk Dillon?'

He immediately sensed that the news was not what we were hoping for and agreed to meet me at the house. We drove to the park and walked a couple of laps with our dog, Dillon. I joked that I could end up with less hair than Liam, but he was not amused. He kept saying that things like this didn't happen to people like us. I assured him they happened to anyone.

He added, 'We've just started to do so well. We've bought a yard.' Liam had recently become the proud owner of business premises. 'The problem with us is that one of us can't survive without the other.' That really broke me in two.

Twelve friends and I had completed the 26.2 mile 'Moon Walk' in our bras for breast cancer the month before. How the hell could this be happening? How had I managed to do that and all the training beforehand if I had breast cancer? Surely, I would have felt ill and had some symptoms. How ironic that I'd raised money for this cause while oblivious to what lay in store for me?

Liam and I went home and tried to put on brave faces. We had a meeting at Ethan's school that evening because he was going on a school trip to France. I also had to swing by work as there was an injured woodpecker that needed syringe feeding and was not doing well.

Liam and I slept exceptionally badly that night. Each time one of us woke up, the other was already awake. I sobbed in Liam's arms like I'd never done before.

She stood in the storm and,
when the wind did not blow her way,
she adjusted her sails

In the morning, Mick the woodpecker (I called him that as he had a red head like Mick Hucknall) was not doing well. I knew he needed to be put to sleep. He couldn't stand and he looked like he was gasping; his beak was continually opening and closing.

I drove to work and was just getting out of the car when Liam rang, asking how I was. I fell to pieces. He announced he was coming to take me home as I wasn't fit for work. I carried Mick into the surgery in a white wire cage and explained to my work colleague, Wendy, that sadly he needed to be euthanised. I didn't take off my sunglasses and started crying. I tried to explain to Wendy about the lump, what the doctor had reported and that I couldn't sleep with worry. She looked shell-shocked and hugged me. With tears running down my face and watery fluid coming down my nose, I made my way out of the door and headed home.

I decided there and then to ring the Spire, a private hospital in Harpenden, to see what they could do. The woman on the end of the phone was so accommodating. She explained that they had a breast-care department and could fit me in that day at 2pm. The consultation, mammogram and ultrasound would cost approximately

£550 and any extras such as biopsies would make it £2200 plus.

I would have sold my soul to have an answer. I rang Liam and he shouted without hesitation, 'Book it!'

We arrived at Spire Hospital well before time. My head was all over the place.

The staff directed me into a changing room and told me to change into a hospital robe. Once again, I fell apart when I was out of Liam's sight. The nurse was very sympathetic; I could tell that she was the perfect person for the job as she was so caring and empathetic.

Whilst I was getting changed, I caught sight of myself in the mirror. My left breast definitely looked slightly different to the right one. Why the hell had I not noticed that before? When I lifted my arm above my head, the difference became more apparent. There was an obvious lump.

I sat down with Liam in the waiting room and flicked through some magazines without reading any of the articles. I was sat bold upright, tense as a coiled spring. Liam kept telling me to relax.

I was called through to see a bespectacled man in his late fifties, Dr Crawley. He was very matter of fact as he explained what was going to happen.

He examined me thoroughly, then sat back down. All through the examination I squeezed the dark-haired nurse Jackie's hand and felt tears running down my cheeks. Dr Crawley confirmed there was definitely a lump; fingers crossed' it might be a cyst as they could grow quite big in a short space of time. He explained that I would need a mammogram and ultrasounds to check if this was the case.

I had both, then a local anaesthetic was injected into my breast. Deep down, I knew this wasn't a cyst that we were dealing with.

Biopsies and fine-needle aspirates were taken from my breast and lymph tissue. I was with a different nurse this time who squeezed my hand and told me how brave I was – it was a blatant lie as I clearly wasn't. She asked me about my job as a veterinary nurse and made conversation about her young German shepherd who had kidney stones.

I clamped my eyes shut the whole way through the procedure; I was shaking with fear and shock. Then I was told to sit with Liam, and I cried my eyes out again. He looked so wide eyed and scared. Jackie the nurse took us to a side room instead of waiting room; I was adamant that I didn't want the other women to see me in that state because it would distress them.

Dr Crawley called me back into his room. He explained that it wasn't a cyst and he thought there was a strong possibility that the lump was cancerous.

We would have to wait seven days for confirmation. He didn't think that there was any lymph node involvement, but we'd have to wait and see. He added that, as I wasn't insured and we were self-funding, he would be happy to see me as an NHS patient, but it would be at the QE2 and Lister Hospital in Hertfordshire instead of my local hospital, the Luton and Dunstable.

He told us that he could have the results the following Tuesday, with a view for surgery on the Thursday. He went on to say that we had already run up a considerable bill; if we continued going private, we would be looking at re-mortgaging the house, so it was a no-brainer to become his

NHS patient. I'd have further to travel each time, but I would have followed that man to the ends of the earth as I had such confidence in his no-nonsense manner.

When I got home, I decided I needed to tell one family member. I chose my sister Donna because she is the eldest and is very calm and logical. She would probably be the best person to deal with this. I rang her and burst into tears as I said that I needed to speak urgently to her face to face. I asked her not to tell a soul and I would be there shortly.

I sat in her living room and explained everything. Donna was dumbfounded but incredibly strong and told me that it was a very treatable cancer. Millie, her thirteen-year-old daughter, came into the room and made a hasty exit when she saw my tear-stained face and bloodshot eyes. I found out afterwards that she thought Liam and I had had a massive falling out.

I know it sounds like a cliché, but I felt like I was in a bad dream. Liam went up to bed around 10pm and I followed an hour later. I decided to sleep with Ethan that night so that I could cuddle my son and be close to him.

Around 3.30am I heard our cat Finnegan meowing continuously as he made his way up the stairs. I jumped out of bed and he dropped a live grey mouse on the landing floor, where it moved around very slowly. I clapped my hands and shouted at Finnegan, and he grabbed the mouse again and ran downstairs into the dining room. There he spat it out under the table then scarpered out of the cat flap at a hundred miles an hour.

The poor mouse was flat out on the floor and there was absolutely no movement. I felt so sorry for it. I closed the dining room door, went upstairs and told Liam to dispose of it in the morning as I couldn't bear to touch it. In the morning, when Liam went down, he shouted, 'There is no mouse!!' I knew then that the little fellow had faked his death and survived by doing so.

Liam said he wasn't having a live mouse running round the house; when he got home from work, he'd put Finnegan in with it to finish the job. I offered Ethan money to try and catch it before he went to school, but he didn't have any luck. When Liam rang later giving out about the mouse, I started crying. I explained to him how the poor mouse had survived when all the odds were stacked against him; he'd even played dead so that he could live. I begged Liam not to let Finnegan kill it because it felt like the mouse was me, trying to survive against the odds.

Liam yelled, 'Jesus, it's only a feckin mouse, but yes, that's fine.' Crazy as it might seem, it was not just a mouse, it was a creature that was determined not to give up. It was my hero.

Everyone wants happiness,
no one wants pain.
But how can you make a rainbow
without a little rain?

I texted my friend Helen after her morning run and asked if she could pop in. She rang me half an hour later and asked if everything was ok as I was off work. I broke down and responded that I just needed to see her.

She kept saying, 'Michelle, please tell me what's wrong.'

I eventually blurted out, 'I may have breast cancer.'

She was round in two minutes, full of apologies for making me say it over the phone. It wasn't her fault – I think I'd really frightened her with my abnormal behaviour. Collette, another friend, called round too. She was very composed when we delivered the news and was a very calming influence because Helen was at a loss what to do or say. As for me, I just kept crying.

I had a hen do coming up that weekend in Liverpool for a very good friend, Philomena. I'd been so looking forward to it. My sisters were all going, and we were going to share a room, so I knew the craic would be great.

Now I realized that it could be a long time before we could all do this again, which made me even more determined to go. This would be the last joyous time we could share before they found out about the shit I was facing.

Fiona, my sister who lives in Ireland, was one of the bridesmaids and the chief organiser. For months we'd been thinking about themes, games and party bags, so I really didn't want to fall at the first hurdle and miss out.

Liam was not at all happy; he was adamant that I shouldn't go. He was worried about the bruising from the biopsies on top of everything else that was going on.

He was furious and even rang Donna to see if she could dissuade me. However, they both knew how obstinate I could be once I'd set my heart on something. He told Donna that he was fuming, and she was in charge of me if anything went wrong.

'I'm going, and that's that!' I shouted at Liam.

'Why the fuck did I marry you?' he shouted back. 'You never ever do a thing I tell you to!'

After a night's sleep, Liam was in better spirits. He rang me and I broke down. I confided that I had to go; I needed to be plain old Michelle for one more weekend before the onslaught of doctor's appointments and hospital visits.

Helen and Collette were very good and kept texting to see how I was. I spoke to one of my work friends, Clare, about my situation. She'd gone through a similar experience but thankfully her lump was harmless. She informed me that in her friendship group of nine women, all but one had had a breast-lump scare at some point. Only one of those girls went on to have treatment for cancer but she was okay now. That really lifted my spirits and I suddenly felt positive.

I went down to Liam's yard and decided to write a letter to the first doctor I'd seen who had coldly informed me that I may have cancer. I made it apparent that it was for her eyes only because I didn't want her reprimanded, just to know how I'd felt. Fortunately, I have a large, supportive network of friends and family but one day someone might enter her consulting room who didn't have that support, who would go home to an empty house and be scared out of their mind as they waited two weeks to be seen by a breast-care specialist.

Dear Dr Calvey

I am writing this letter not on my behalf but on behalf of the patients that you will be seeing in the future.

I came to an appointment with you on Monday as I had discovered a large lump in my breast on the Saturday prior. I was extremely worried and told no one. The first time I even mentioned the lump was when I spoke to the receptionist at your surgery. Just saying it aloud made it seem real and scared the hell out of me.

I explained how worried I was, and I said I was more than happy to see the first doctor that was available – be it at my own surgery or one of their branches. The receptionist very kindly booked me an appointment with you, as she wanted to ensure I saw a female doctor.

Once I walked into your room, I explained how the lump had only just been noticed and how concerned I was. You asked when my last period was – when I said I couldn't remember, possibly a few weeks ago – you said it was 'disgusting that a woman does not keep note of her periods' – that you should always keep a log. You then went on to rant about why was I at your surgery and not my usual one and continued to complain that this was happening a lot of times. You even went on to complain that the blue paper towel hadn't been pulled down on the examining bed from the previous staff who had used the room. You examined me and told me there was a four-inch lump across my breast and, due to the sudden onset, you would refer me. I broke down then and still you were as cold as ice. I felt you thought I was a major inconvenience to you.

Maybe you were having a bad day; maybe you were frustrated that I was an extra one on your list; maybe you just don't like your job anymore, and maybe you have been in the job too long and have lost your bedside manner. Whatever the case may be, I felt so let down by you as a) a doctor and b) a woman.

I am writing this letter not for an apology, not even an acknowledgement, but just to let you know that human beings have feelings and when you have someone in your room who even thinks that they may have the dreaded C word (I still can't bring myself to say it), you could treat them with the compassion that they deserve.

Regards

Who knows if it ever made any difference, but I felt I was back in some sort of control. I would like to think she was more sympathetic to the next worried person who tentatively walks into her consulting room.

I went for lunch with Helen, who was quite startled at how upbeat I was. Nothing or no one was going to dampen my spirits. Collette came round later to put gel nails on my toes and fingers to make them look good for the hen do. I also wanted them to look glam when I looked down on them after my surgery; it might be the only pampering I'd have for a while, and I wanted to embrace it.

Whilst she painted my nails, I set Ethan, Orla and her friends, Rosie and Aoibhan, the task of trying to catch the mouse to release him back into the wild. I heard screams as it scurried past them and ran through their legs. Finally, after about an hour, I heard cheers as the elusive mouse was caught.

Rosie thought he was very sweet, named him Gerry and asked if she could keep him. I texted her mum, Cathy, who told me in no uncertain terms to feck off. Gerry was ceremoniously released into the neighbour's garden.

The following night, Finnegan came through the cat flap with a dead mouse in his jaws. I like to think it was not 'our Gerry' and he is living a great life with his wife and kids.

Friends are like stars,
they come and go,
but the ones that stay
are the ones that glow

Liverpool was fantastic and I never regretted for a minute my decision to go, although it would have been preferable to leave my faulty boob in a drawer at home and forget about it. The only dampener on the weekend was when I found that my camera battery was flat. I'd been adamant I wanted some great photos as memories, and I'd spent ages shopping for a battery charger. I finally bought one which didn't work, so that was a real shame. For some reason at that point, my photos and memories seemed more poignant than ever.

Before we went out that night, Liam rang to say that his cheque book had been cloned and someone had taken about £4,000 from his business account.

'It's only money. We'll get it sorted when I get back,' I said.

Liam ranted on and on and finally I snapped back, 'Jesus, money is fuck all to what I am going through!' I slammed down the phone and ran to the en suite in the room I was sharing with my three sisters. I knelt on the floor and sobbed my eyes out.

My sisters banged on the door, asking me what was wrong. I shouted back that I wanted one weekend to enjoy and Liam was ringing me about lost company money. I didn't need this when I was away to enjoy myself and there was nothing I could do about it. I found out later that my sisters thought my behaviour was uncharacteristic, but they didn't question it.

Liam texted me shortly afterwards to tell me how sorry he was, and he hoped I'd have a great weekend. I didn't respond though I should have done; Liam was trying to talk about normal things and I was hell bent on not listening. I'd been blindsided by the possible cancer diagnosis, and I had tunnel vision.

I purposely left my phone behind when I went out. When I got back that night, there was a text from Liam apologising. I rang him the next morning very early and he sounded so relieved to hear from me, God love him.

He apologised again and said he needed his right-hand woman beside him because he couldn't cope otherwise.

Philomena was the perfect hen and did everything that was asked of her. We were blessed with a great group of females. I did have a little wobble at the bar when a song came on, and I only just held it together. Donna turned and asked how I was doing and I felt myself welling up. I said that I was going to sneak off home at 11pm but in the end I managed to last the distance. The pub was doing a promotion with double shots of top shelf drinks, but they weren't even touching the sides!

Liam rang me numerous times during the weekend. Joanna commented, 'Jesus, Liam doesn't cope very well when you're away."

Poor Liam; he was only looking out for me and ensuring no harm came to me, but I suppose to everyone else it looked like he was never off the phone.

Saturday night we had a ball. The theme was black trousers, jackets, bow ties and white shirts, so our gang looked very classy.

We started off with a jiving lesson from Josie. We danced like lunatics and drank our bodyweight in wine and Porn-Star Martinis. We even had a big old Irish singsong in a glass-topped roof bar where we ate a lovely meal.

I spoke to one of Philomena's cousins and explained that I was awaiting cancer results. I didn't know her, but she seemed lovely and it felt good to offload to a stranger. I looked at my sisters' faces as they danced and laughed and felt a lump in my throat at the upset I would cause when I revealed my news.

As the night wore on, more and more of the hen party made their way home. Soon the last two women standing were my sister Fiona and me. As we were walking home, Fiona turned to me and asked, 'Is everything okay? You seemed to lose your sparkle in the last pub.'

I told her I was fine, but I sounded half-hearted. She kept insisting something was wrong and she wanted to know.

By now the heavens had opened and it was pouring down. I finally relented and said, 'Okay, Fiona, I have something to tell you.'

She looked at me with fear and panic etched across her face and shouted back, 'No, no, I don't want to know!' and marched ahead of me.

'I think I may have breast cancer,' I whispered.

Fiona stopped dead in her tracks and walked back to me. 'No! no! You haven't, you haven't!' she screamed.

When I explained that I'd found a lump, Fiona roared back, 'That doesn't mean anything. You haven't even been to a doctor. It could be anything.'

I explained that I had seen a doctor and had numerous tests done, including a mammogram, ultrasound and biopsies.

Fiona started to sob; it broke my heart to see her like that. She kept saying, 'You can't have cancer. You're our rock. No! You haven't got it.'

By now the rain was belting down in biblical proportions and we were walking aimlessly round the streets of Liverpool with no destination in mind. A drunken lad sidled over to us, thought better of it when he saw how despondent and dispirited we were and had the good grace to walk off elsewhere.

Fiona punished herself, crying and saying, 'Oh my God, you wanted to go for a sleep earlier and I just dragged you round Liverpool. How could I be so selfish?'

'Jesus,' I said, 'you weren't to know.'

We hugged, sobbed and talked into the early hours of the morning before we walked back to the hotel and headed to bed. I knew I'd have to tell my other sister Joanna in the morning.

'I am so looking forward to poached eggs on toast,' were Joanna's first words when she woke up. I decided to let her enjoy her breakfast before I told her. I didn't go downstairs to join them.

Once everyone was all back in the room, cases packed, I decided it was the time. 'Joanna, I'm having tests done for breast cancer.'

Joanna looked stunned and said, 'God! What? How?'

I told her and she seemed optimistic that everything would be okay.

We planned to tell my brother Kieran that night. He is the baby of the family, younger than me by fourteen years, and a very welcome surprise after four girls. He was out for a meal with Mum, so it was put on hold for another day.

I needed to tell all my immediate family members. Donna had initially said she would tell them on my behalf, but I thought it only fair that I told them face to face. The following evening, I picked up Joanna and Donna and headed to Mum's house. My Mum and Dad had separated years ago but still get on very well; in fact better than when they were married.

Anyone who knows my mum will tell you what a proud, fiercely loyal, independent and strong Irish woman she is. She protects us like a lioness protects their young; God help anyone who upsets us. Mum will forgive them, but I know they will always have a 'red mark' against their name.

I really was dreading this as I know she is such a worrier.

She beamed when she saw us all at her door and said, 'How lovely to see ye all.'

We marched into her living room and I spoke first. 'Mum, sit down. I have something I need to tell you.'

She immediately looked scared and raised her hands to her head. Donna said gently, 'Mum, please listen and be calm.'

'I'm having tests at the moment for breast cancer,' I whispered.

Mum went white; she looked like someone had pulled the stuffing out of her. She was silent for a few seconds and then the questions flooded out. She was stunned when she learned how long ago the lump had been found. She said she would sell her house and pay whatever it took to have me fighting fit again.

I explained that the doctor was happy to see me as an NHS patient, and I would be getting the results of my tests the following day. I begged her to stay away from her medical books and not go on the internet – I didn't want her Googling anything that would worry her more. Mum is a nightmare with her medical dictionaries, and sometimes she assumes the worst when it is something trivial. We always make a joke of this, but she sometimes thinks she knows more than the health professionals.

I thought I'd wait another day before I told my dad and my brother. There was no point worrying them until I knew what I was dealing with.

I rang my sister-in-law Yvonne in Ireland; she had fought breast cancer years before and overcome it. She would be the person I would pick for a 2am phonecall – she has always been there for me. Yvonne is such an inspirational woman. She had also overcome the demon drink and is now a respected AA councillor in Northern Ireland. She has walked a hard path, but has such a calming, spiritual nature because of it. I have such faith in Yvonne, who is my friend first, and sister-in law, second. She was truly gobsmacked, but she was so good to talk to. I was all over the show on the phone, one minute completely calm then sobbing uncontrollably.

She turned her can'ts into cans
and her dreams into plans

The day of the results came. We had to drop Ethan off on his school trip at 4am so we didn't sleep well. He was so excited, God love him.

Afterwards we went back to bed for a couple of hours. Our friend Brian picked up Orla for school, and we made our arduous journey to the QE2 Hospital for the results.

The waiting room was packed with women and their 'plus ones'.

I pretended to flick through a magazine, but I couldn't help the tears rolling down my face. I thought no one had noticed until a young lad handed me a tissue without uttering a word. It was such a simple gesture, but it meant the world to me. I smiled at him and hoped the woman sitting beside him, presumably his mum, would get good news.

We were finally called through. Dr Crawley announced that the laboratory findings were conclusive: it was cancer.

Surgery would go ahead first thing on Thursday to remove the lump with wide margins. He would also remove all my lymph nodes in my left armpit since the results showed up that there was involvement there, too.

I felt unbelievably crushed. I'd thought for one tiny second that he might say it was a mistake, it was actually a lipoma (a fatty lump), and I could get back to living a normal life again. I remembered one time at work when a yellow Labrador came in for surgery on a very suspect lump; it turned out to be a lipoma and we were all so relieved. For some bizarre reason, I thought this might happen me too.

Nobody can ever properly explain how you feel when the doctor utters those words to you. You feel like you are on a runaway train that's been derailed and is taking everyone and everything you hold dear and scattering them like skittles. A million-zillion thoughts go through your head at 100mph and none of them are favourable. Your mortality flashes before you; in those fleeting minutes, I had all but buried myself.

We were taken to a small room where the breast-care nurse explained the procedure and what to expect afterwards. She handed me leaflet after leaflet, bombarding me with information about how to deal with cancer, lymphoedema, chemo, surgery, telling your kids. She informed me that after surgery I could never have blood pressure or bloods taken from my left arm, or any injections into it. It would need to be protected from scratches, bites and injuries because I would have no lymph nodes in it to drain away infection. This could lead to a lifelong, irreversible condition known as lymphoedema, which would result in me wearing a compression bandage at all times to reduce the swelling, and my arm would feel like a dead weight. My beloved job as a veterinary nurse would now be very risky.

I remember looking out of the window at the people below and wishing I could dive into their bodies – anything to be out of mine.

There was so much to take in. I was being propelled into a foreign world when I yearned for the comfort and familiarity of my old one.

Nearly six years later, those leaflets are still gathering dust above the kitchen cupboards out of my sight. I'm a great believer in dealing with problems once they arise. That may seem ignorant, but it is my way of coping.

I had MRSA swabs taken, and my blood pressure, weight and height were recorded. Once again, I sobbed all the way through. I rang Joanna, told her my devastating news and she broke down. I asked her to let Donna and Mum know then rang Fiona, who was absolutely distraught.

Liam kept saying, 'I wasn't expecting this. This is a lot more complicated than I thought.'

We were both starving so we drove to a cafe in Harpenden for a very late breakfast. We met two sisters from Liam's hometown in Donegal. One of them had had her fortieth birthday the weekend before and was explaining that her eyelids were red because she'd had an allergic reaction to the false eyelashes she'd worn. She must have thought I had some sort of allergy too, as my eyes were bright red. They were a welcome distraction, but the ugly elephant was sitting firmly in the room.

That evening I rang my friend Claire and burst into tears. She came round quick as a flash. She later gave me a holy Virgin Mary pendant, which I tied onto a piece of garden string and put round my neck.

I needed to tell my dad, so Liam and I headed to his house. Dad is a softly spoken, kind Irish gentleman with a cracking sense of humour, and he lit up when he saw us. We sat down and I revealed my news.

He jumped off the settee and said, 'Oh Lord Jesus.' He looked devastated. This was my dad, and he just didn't know what to say or how to act around me. He started talking about his drill and couldn't make eye contact. He babbled on for a while, talking about everything and anything but not what he has just heard from us.

I went to see my brother Kieran and his girlfriend, Michelle. Donna and Joanna were meant to meet me there, but they were stuck in traffic.

I walked in and just came straight out with it. Kieran never opened his mouth; he looked like a man in shock.

Michelle, who is a nurse, kept talking and talking. God love her, she said how good it was that they were acting so quickly, and I was going to a great hospital. She jumped up, hugged me and repeated everything she'd just said over again.

The last few days had drained me so much mentally, but I knew I had a lot more to face as my dreaded surgery was now only two days away.

I was brought up a Catholic and I pray every night without fail. After I was diagnosed, I really embraced my faith again.

Helen had been to Ireland and bought me loads of St Anthony relics and candles, as I have great belief in him. Her mum, Della, arranged for me to have two masses a day for a year in Knock, County Mayo. Yvonne rang and informed me that her friends from the AA sessions whom she mentored had assured her that they would all be lighting candles and sending me prayers. She said that Donegal and Derry would be 'lit up' from all the well- wishers' candles. That really gave me a lot of comfort and I felt humbled. My phone resembled a hotline with so many messages of support.

Collette came round and removed my beautiful gel nails because I couldn't wear nail varnish whilst under an anaesthetic. I felt that the cancer had even taken that away from me.

The night before the operation, I told Orla. We knew we couldn't hide it from our daughter as I would be gone for a few days. We just said I had a lump which needed to be removed. She was very tearful and said she didn't want anyone to hurt me. I asked her to be strong – I needed her to be the woman of the house and keep her dad in check.

Orla came shopping with me to buy toiletries for my hospital stay; I wanted her to feel involved and included, and she seemed grateful for that. She stayed the night at her friend's house because we had to be at the hospital for 7am.

Fiona sent me a beautiful email with an article she had found about an eagle and a chicken in a storm and how they both approached it. It had me in tears.

Imagine a chicken in a chicken yard. She's scratching in the dirt looking for something to eat. It's hot, dusty and dirty. Now imagine an eagle. He's sitting high on a cliff, his sharp eyes scanning the valley in search of food. Finally, imagine a storm coming. Dark clouds looming in the distance. Rolling thunder and the threat of hard wind and rain just moments away.

27

What do you think these two birds will do in the face of the storm? They're both birds but they face the storm in radically different ways. They both have wings and feathers and beaks. But the main difference between an eagle and a chicken is how they think. It's what's inside that counts as much as what's outside.

The chicken will immediately become worried. She'll run in circles and flap her wings. Of course, she won't actually fly, but she'll flap and cluck and run for the chicken house and the company of all the other scared chickens. She'll try to get to shelter so she can stay out of the approaching storm.

Now what about the eagle? The eagle won't run, and he won't cluck and make a fuss. He'll actually turn his face into the storm, feeling the strong wind on his face. Then, when the time is right, he'll spread his wings, leap off his perch, and fly directly into the violence of the storm. With his wings outstretched, he'll catch the violent updrafts caused by the storm and be immediately swept up above the clouds and into the bright sunshine. He'll remain above the clouds until the storm blows over and the skies become calm.

Michelle, I definitely know which bird you are.

Xxxxxxxxxxxxxxxxx

Hand on heart, I honestly felt as vulnerable and as weak as a newly hatched chicken – nothing like an eagle.

*Sometimes the thing that you fear
the most is the very thing
that will set you free.*

Liam and I didn't sleep well; we were both too anxious. In the morning there were two envelopes in our letterbox. One was from Cathy and Brian, wishing me good luck; the other had a picture of a mouse on the front.

When I opened it, in shaky writing, it wished me the best of luck from Gerry the mouse that had survived the cat attack. That set me off and I cried and laughed at such a lovely kind thought.

Mum came round with some new pyjamas and we all set off to the Lister Hospital. Once we arrived at reception, I was called through but Liam and Mum could come no further. I removed my necklace and placed the holy relic round my mother's neck so she could wear it during my operation. I felt so alone, small and extremely fragile.

I sobbed through a series of tests. There were elderly women in there with not a peep out of them, and there was I bawling my eyes out. Through the dividing curtain I heard a lady laughing and joking with the nurses. She sounded so brave and upbeat as she told them how a lump under her armpit went ignored and she now needed a bone-marrow transplant. She revealed that she was an older mum and had a four-year-old son who was autistic. I wanted to run to the end of the ward with my hands over my ears so that I couldn't hear her, but at the same time I was rooted to the spot by her courage and positivity. I really wanted to pull back the curtain and hug her, put a face to this woman, but of course I couldn't invade her privacy.

I texted my family on WhatsApp to say the song of the day was Avici, 'Wake Me Up When It's All Over', as that was exactly what I wanted: to stay asleep until the operation, and possible chemotherapy, radiotherapy and treatment were all behind me.

The registrar went over my health record and declared that I would be fourth on the list and should have surgery around 11am.

I was distressed and said that Dr Crawley had promised me I would be first on his list. The registrar apologised but said that was not the case. I was crying, saying I wanted it over. Honest to God, I hadn't stopped crying since the twenty-third of June; they would need at least five litres of fluids to replace the tears I'd shed.

Finally Dr Crawley came round. He told me to take no notice of the list and reassured me I would be first. I could have kissed him there and then.

I was taken to the prep room, where they inserted an IV catheter. They gave me an intravenous injection, which they said would be like drinking a large glass of wine. I don't remember anything after that.

When I came round, I was shaking uncontrollably. The nurse gently informed me that I'd had the operation. I couldn't believe it.

They kept putting more and more blankets on me but the shaking was not from the cold but delight at having come through the first stage.

I asked the nurse if I could look at the lump – I wanted to see the bastard squatter that had come into my body uninvited and turned mine and my family's life upside down – but it was already on its way to the laboratory together with nineteen of my lymph nodes. I had a drain placed in my chest to drain away the fluid from my surgery site.

For some reason I had to stay in recovery for hours before they could get a bed ready on the ward. Liam kept texting me; he was outside the door with my mum and dad, and they were desperate to see me. I wasn't in the slightest bit annoyed because I was so elated the op was over and the relief was immense. They finally let Mum in to see me and she was so relieved, God love her. Liam and Dad had to go home to collect Orla from school. Liam knew she would be worried.

The wards were so overstretched that I was finally taken to a private one. It was lovely. I had an enormous room all to myself. I was laughing and joking to my mum that I was going to have my own pool, and she was so gullible she believed me. In typical Mum-fashion, she unpacked my suitcase and set about organising my room. Liam arrived shortly after with Orla and Mum left us alone to catch up. Donna and Joanna came to visit me after that.

I felt so drained the following day that I could hardly summon up the energy for my visitors: Dad, Mum and Michelle. The nurses had been doing hourly checks on my blood pressure, oxygen saturation and temperature during the night and it had caught up on me. When Liam and Orla came, I could hardly keep my eyes open.

Ethan was due back around midnight the next night and kept texting me with updates of where he was, as they were slightly delayed. In the end, I texted him to say my phone was playing up and he would need to text Liam – I was so exhausted but scared of falling asleep and missing his messages.

The weather that night was the craziest I've ever seen. My room lit up with the lightning and the rain belted down. The window was slightly ajar as it had been stuffy earlier, and the blind was jumping in the window. I felt very vulnerable, like I was in a war zone, as the storm raged outside.

Claire sent me a photo of her daughter on her prom night. That really hit me so hard. Lying in bed, I feared that I might never get to see my kids dressed up in their prom outfits.

I rang Liam at 1.30am to make sure Ethan had got home okay. Liam put him on the phone and my son sounded so small and childlike on the other end of the line. I knew immediately that he knew. He asked fearfully, 'Are you okay, Mum?' and his voice was barely audible.

'I'm fine,' I replied.

He told me how shocked he was to hear I was in hospital and then he broke down.

I cried too and said, 'Please, Ethan, don't cry or you will set me off.'

'I'm sorry,' he answered. I could imagine him trying to 'man up' and that broke my heart. He was only fourteen years old. He ended the phone call by telling me he loved me and was looking forward to seeing me the next day.

The next day Orla had a Gaelic football tournament. I was determined that she would still play in it and visit me in the evening instead. Joanna and Mum came to visit me in the afternoon. Joanna brought an array of nail polishes as she wanted to paint my toes to try and cheer me up. Mum had about twenty different punnets of fruit for me, and a small cuddly monkey that she'd got free with the teabags. It seemed a very suitable gift because he was wearing a dressing gown like me. On closer examination, I laughed when I noticed he had two different-sized eyes; it seemed quite fitting as I was now a bit lopsided too! I named him Steve (after the Stevenage hospital) and he now comes with me as my lucky mascot each time surgery is needed.

Kieran came shortly afterwards and he was like Mary Poppins, digging stuff out of his bag. I had flowers, nuts, fruit and a magazine. Yvonne had posted a large package from Ireland containing some gorgeous pyjamas, a guardian angel poem, a little guardian angel frame and lots of holy relics from Medigore. She'd thought so carefully about everything and I appreciated it so much.

I struggled with the drain protruding from my body; I couldn't bear to look at it or at my op site. I found it hard to manoeuvre my arm because the incision went across my left breast and along my armpit. I couldn't even contemplate showering; I knew my disgust at seeing a foreign body sticking out of me would turn my stomach. When the nurses came to empty my drain I turned away, put on my headphones, turned up the volume full blast and listened to whatever was on telly.

I refused to look when I got my daily injections of heparin, which were given to reduce the risk of blood clots. I did manage to walk round the hospital corridors a few times carrying my drain, which I covered up with an incontinence pad to prevent me seeing it. I must have looked demented, walking the white-walled corridors with a gaping night gown, wild hair, surgical socks and a drainage bag in my hand. I felt like Jack Nicholson from *One Flew Over the Cuckoo's Nest.* Indeed, Orla informed me after she took a very unflattering photo of me that I resembled Elvis when he was high on drugs.

I perspire lots, and it was horrendous not being able to shower, apply deodorant or change my gown. I had never felt so sweaty in my life and I was beginning to smell like a rabbit hutch. When Liam came later with Ethan and Orla, I could see that Ethan was uncomfortable and taken aback at seeing his mum lying in a hospital bed. He massaged my head and talked me through his school trip. I was so glad he was home. The nights and days were so long, and I lived for visiting hours.

Finally, on the Sunday, the nurse came round, removed my drain and said I could go home. I was so relieved. I rang Liam and asked him to pick me up in an hour and a half to give me time to try and shower and change. My op site was covered with large plasters, thank God, so I couldn't see it. I one-handedly managed to wash my hair and shower and the relief was immense. I felt so clean and fresh.

Liam and the kids came. It was so lovely to leave the hospital and head to the comfort of my own home, even though the staff had been truly amazing.

My armpit was painful after the surgery; it even hurt to scratch the back of my head, shampoo or comb my hair. Dressing and undressing were excruciating as there was so much pain when I extended my arm.

Here's to strong women:
may we know them,
may we be them,
may we raise them

My house was like a florist on my return. My good friends, Beatrice and Wendy, and the 'Reservoir Dogs' (the ladies that I'd done the Moonwalk with) had filled it with flowers. They had also purchased an afternoon tea voucher for the Mansion House at Luton Hoo, so I was completely spoilt.

At a later date, Laura (another Moonwalker) came round with an enormous hamper from all the Moonwalkers with everything you could think of for me to pamper myself again. We headed to my mum's for a roast dinner after my hospital return, which I devoured. I could feel Mum observing me the whole time, watching every mouthful I took. She thought I didn't notice. It made me laugh as she put every vegetable she could think of on my plate. She was going to do anything in her power to build me up again.

The following day, we went to Joanna's. She cooked a delicious curry, which I'd raved about in the past, and my family were all there.

As time went on, it felt like there was this huge elephant in the room and everyone was afraid to mention the C-word.

We were talking about everything and anything just to avoid it.

At one point I felt like I couldn't breathe. Mum wanted to drop off her sick note later that evening, as she was unable to work once I'd been diagnosed. I jumped up and said I wanted to go with her and I headed out the front door. Everyone looked at me. I felt like I was drowning.

When I got into Mum's car, I broke down and sobbed. I didn't want to do this in front of my mum because it scared her. She cried her eyes out and said she would move heaven and earth whilst there was breath in her body to have me well again.

I cried for about five minutes and then I was fine. What the feck was happening to me? I was crying morning, noon and night. I cried for what lay ahead for me; I cried for the impact this had on my family; I cried about the needles, of which I have a deep fear, the chemo, the radiation and possibly more surgery. I cried for my easy, carefree, normal life that seemed a lifetime ago.

The two weeks waiting for the results were the longest I had spent in my life. I became very superstitious, reading into things that had never bothered me before. I wanted to be surrounded by good omens; even silly things like beating the traffic lights might mean good news. Every time I saw a lone magpie, I would be sure to salute it and say, "Hello Mr Magpie, how's your wife and kids" Stupid things like throwing rubbish in the bin had hidden meanings for me: if it landed in the bin, I'd get the all-clear and if it landed on the floor, I would interpret it to be bad news.

Everything else seemed irrelevant. When people moaned about mundane things, like the cost of something or a silly argument they'd had, I felt like screaming at them and telling them that, bad as things seemed, at least they hadn't been told they might have cancer. It's such a horrible word, that automatically makes you think the worst. Headlines in newspapers about people who had died from cancer seemed to jump off the page at me as if preparing me for a bad outcome and taunting me. I saw hearses and heard heart-breaking news on the TV. I saw the local hospice van pull out on the road, and immediately interpreted that as another bad omen.

The night before my I got my results, I watched Orla effortlessly doing headstands and cartwheels in the park. It was such a simple thing.

I so wished that I could move my arm as flexibly as she could and felt demoralised that it felt so useless. I'd been guarding it after surgery as it was so sore and painful to move. I explained my frustrations to Yvonne about how I wished I could do cartwheels and handstands.

She laughed and declared, 'Have you ever done hand stands and cartwheels before?'

'No.'

'Then why the hell do you want to do them now?' she asked. It was a very true statement. She went on to say that after her surgery, she'd wanted to wear strapless summer dresses until she realised she'd never wore them before – so why did she want to wear them now?

Liam noticed that I had become a lot more expressive with my hands when explaining things. I suppose it was another sign of anxiety, something I'd never suffered from before. Fiona had flown over from Ireland with her two kids; she wanted to be there for me, too. I knew it hadn't been easy to pack up and come over at the last minute, and I am forever grateful to her for being there for me.

She had arranged with my mum to visit the nuns of St Claire's, and I decided at the last minute that I wanted to go with them. We arrived at the convent, which was beautifully set in a cul de sac. We walked through a tranquil garden with a pond; eye-catching, colourful flowers bloomed all round it and I felt immediately at peace.

A little nun introduced herself as Sister Antoinette and linked arms with my mum as she spoke about the garden and its peacefulness.

This simple gesture made the tears spring into my eyes. Bloody hell, I needed to hold myself together.

We were introduced to another nun, Sister Kathleen, in a little prayer room with a large circular window that looked on to the lovingly cared for garden.

It really was a slice of heaven. Sister Kathleen explained about when they bought the house, the arguments after viewing other properties, and how this house ticked all the right boxes. Her face lit up and she was so animated as she recalled those fond memories. We were given rosary beads from Medigore, and she blessed all the paraphernalia that I'd brought with me. Sister Kathleen read out a prayer and we recited the rosary. I was so glad I'd come because I do believe that miracles can happen. I was also given a simple wooden cross which she called a 'comforting cross'. It fitted perfectly into the palm of my hand. This cross was to become an integral part of my hospital kit bag.

I felt immeasurably fearful and welled up whenever I was shown an act of kindness. It was so overwhelming.

That night we went out for an Indian meal with my family. My impending results were not mentioned but the atmosphere, along with my heart, felt heavy.

Fiona was flying back to Ireland the next morning and I broke down as I said goodbye to her.

Look for something positive in each day,
even if sometimes you have to
look a little harder.

The morning of the results came. I bathed, dressed and picked up my mum because I was also attending my friend Julie's dad's funeral that day at 11.30am.

I decided to go to the crematorium and the pub afterwards with the funeral crowd – anything to keep my mind off what lay ahead.

I could only stay a short time at the pub, and I felt bad leaving my friend in her sorrow, but the hours were ticking by. I dropped Mum home; she was very tearful and kept hugging me.

For the last fortnight, I'd kept saying that I didn't care what the results were as long as I didn't have to undergo surgery again. That day I changed my mind; if it was meant to be, I would have to go with it, still hoping to God that they'd taken enough margins from the op site.

I went home to Liam at 2.30pm. He was not happy; he felt that I should have only gone to the funeral mass and straight home to him.

He was also going mad with worry, wondering what my results would be. We had a row, I ended up roaring at him to fuck off, and we drove to my appointment in silence. I couldn't believe that this feckin C word was coming between us and making us both behave so irrationally.

The waiting room was packed, standing room only, filled with women and their plus ones. There were a couple of women who'd obviously gone through chemo and were bald or had hair sprouting back like newly hatched fledglings. In a strange sort of way, I felt envious that they'd already gone through it and started to come out the other side.

It soon became apparent that our 3.30pm appointment was not running to time. I had to keep texting Mum, my family and Yvonne; I knew they were clock-watching and pacing the floor waiting for news. We finally were called through at 6pm. My legs felt like they were going to give way during the walk to Dr Crawley's room.

Dr Crawley didn't pull any punches: fourteen of the nineteen lymph nodes contained cancerous cells. He did say that the lump was four centimetres, not the four inches as the original doctor had said. However, enough healthy tissue hadn't been removed from the breast lump so I would have to undergo more surgery, possibly a lumpectomy or a mastectomy.

I felt deflated, like this wasn't real. I'd been convinced that the news would be more favourable, and this was a lot worse than I'd imagined.

I remained completely composed during the consultation, even though the rug had been pulled from under my feet. I felt like I was floating round the room rather than sitting in the chair.

We went into a room with the breast-care nurse, who'd been present during the consultation, and I fell apart. She said that in my case, she'd recommend a large glass of wine when I got home to try and help me feel slightly calmer.

An appointment was made for 29th July to go through my chemo plan. The nurse talked about cold capping, a process where you have your head frozen to something crazy like minus thirty-seven degrees. It is not for everyone as it's intensely painful. I asked if I would definitely lose my hair if I didn't cold cap, and she said that I would. My voice didn't even sound like my own when I asked about my eyebrows. The answer was exactly the same.

The nurse asked me to do some more exercises with my left arm as they weren't happy with my mobility after surgery. We were told to go ahead with our holiday to Spain as planned. The chemo regime that I would receive would be called FEC-T – I did think Feck C would have been more fitting. The letters were abbreviations for the names of the drugs that would be pumped into my body.

I would have six chemos at three-week intervals. The first three would be a combination of three different drugs, and the last three sessions would be one drug. All of them would introduce different, horrible side effects.

It was a lot to take in. I rang Mum first and broke down as I asked her to let everyone else know. She was in bits and assured me that she would inform the rest of the family.

I rang my friend Cathy, who'd taken care of Orla for the last few days and broke down to her. I said I wanted to pick up Orla from the school disco as I'd missed dropping her there because my appointment was late.

I rang Yvonne and sobbed uncontrollably. Yvonne kept shouting, 'Listen to me! Listen to me! They've offered you treatment – that's great. Many a woman has walked into that room and been offered nothing.'

When I told her of the fourteen lymph nodes that were affected, she said, 'Yes, but there are five that aren't affected.' It was then that I realised I'd been focusing on the glass half empty and not half full. Yvonne has a way of making even bad things sound positive.

When we walked in the door, Ethan had freshly baked scones waiting for me with hand-whipped cream in the fridge. The kitchen was spotless. I found out later that when Cathy had come to pick an outfit for Orla's disco, my kitchen had looked like a bomb site and Ethan had point blank refused her offer to help. She explained how close to tears she was at his kindness.

Ethan kept asking what the news was, but I couldn't tell him as we had to pick up Orla. He turned to me when we got to the school playground and asked, 'Is it cancer?'

I looked at him and felt my heart would break. I couldn't lie to him; it simply wasn't fair. 'I will tell you everything when Orla goes to bed,' I whispered. The look in his eyes made me painfully aware that he knew.

Once Orla had gone to sleep, I explained everything to Ethan about the chemo. He looked seriously worried and asked would it be safe for me to stay at home whilst I went through it. He was petrified of coughing or sneezing near me.

He had tons of questions and I answered them all as honestly as I could. He kissed me and told me he loved me.

I didn't think that Orla was ready to deal with it yet. She was only ten years old, whilst her older brother was four years older (to the day).

44

I told Ethan that he could speak to or confide in any of my family if he needed someone to talk to. I explained that some days I might appear cross or tearful, but we'd get there in the end; 2015 would consist of lots of hospital visits, so 2016 would be our year.

Once Ethan had gone to bed, my family came round and we talked and talked. After they left, Helen called round and we talked into the early hours. I shed a few tears and had a few glasses of prosecco. Helen christened me with my new nickname, Tiny Tears. I'd definitely earned it.

Cathy organised a meal at her house for the next day for a group of us with our husbands and kids. She had planned to cancel it after learning of my results but I persuaded her to let it go ahead. It was something I needed at that moment.

It was such a brilliant night. We ate al fresco and the drink and conversation flowed. Liam and the kids left before me – Helen and I were the last to leave. There was talk from me about starting a singsong, but Cathy and Brian had the good sense to send me home!

I went to collect Orla from school a few days later and her teacher asked me for a quick word. She explained that Orla was incredibly tearful because she knew what was happening to me. Ethan had told her after she'd questioned him about it. Unbeknown to me, she had uncovered some cancer literature hidden in my bedroom drawer. Her teacher went on to say that Orla loved Ethan and wanted him there when she was so distressed. She didn't want to worry me.

My heart felt like it would break in two. I felt helpless; I didn't know she had carried this burden to school. I was so proud of them both for trying to be so grown up and confiding in one another, and gutted that they had to deal with this shit.

We had a good talk. Orla revealed that she absolutely hated the word 'cancer' and she wanted it to be called Bob. She yelled that if Bob was a person, she'd 'beat the crap out of him'. Her words, not mine.

Our holiday was looming closer. I really didn't feel like going, but the kids and Liam were excited. This could be our last holiday for a while, so I decided we needed to enjoy it and make it fun for everyone.

We had a great time, but the weather was unbearably hot. We didn't have air conditioning and my nights were restless; even with no blankets, sweat was still pouring out of every pore. During the daytime I stayed in the apartment whilst Liam and the kids swam in the outdoor pool. I managed to swim a few times early in the morning or the evening because the doctor had told me to protect myself from the sun. I pushed myself because I needed to get my left arm moving properly again; it was really hard, but I felt better for it.

We had a great time eating out and driving to different places. One day, whilst shopping in a large supermarket, my song, 'Wake Me Up When It's All Over' came over the speakers and I stood there, rooted to the spot. It hit me big time, reminding me of what I was heading back to; Spain was merely a distraction. I felt my eyes welling up but I managed to contain myself before the kids saw. Although it was a good holiday, I felt like a dirty black cloud was looming over our heads.

The flight back was only two hours but seemed longer. Orla burst into tears and sobbed about my impending chemo. I also started crying; my throat felt like it was going to explode with the lump in it. Liam kept looking at us in a panic. He and Ethan were across the aisle and he was at a loss as to why the two 'women' in his life were bawling their eyes out and he couldn't do anything about it.

If you obey all the rules,
you miss all the fun.

I had to undergo a CT scan at the Lister Hospital to make sure there were no secondaries and got chatting to a girl in the waiting room who was with her partner. She explained that I would have to drink a jug of fluid that tasted like Pernod, then have a cannula placed in my vein through which they would inject a dye into my veins. In my head I started to panic as I'd had no idea it involved an intravenous cannula.

The girl was so friendly. It transpired that she had skin cancer resulting from a mole on her leg. She'd had surgery but was being monitored extremely closely, and she was to undergo surgery to have the lymph nodes removed from inside her leg. This was a tricky procedure and meant a drain would be inserted for two weeks.

We chatted about how scary everything was. She mentioned she was going on holiday to Tenerife in a few weeks and she'd been too worried to enjoy it. Her partner didn't speak much, but every so often she reached out and squeezed his hand like she was reassuring him that everything would be okay.

The nurse had difficulty locating a vein, so a doctor had to insert it. By the time that had happened, my new friend had gone, and I cursed myself for not getting her number. I felt like I had missed out on a chance to connect with someone who was in the same boat as me. My CT scan went ahead and Liam and I headed home after a long, drawn-out day. I was told I'd have the results for Monday.

I rang the Lister a few days later to see if they could find the name of the girl in the waiting room but, because of patient confidentiality, they couldn't give me any details. I left my number with the nurse and asked if there was any way she could get the girl to contact me. I felt I'd missed an opportunity to be with someone who knew how I was feeling. I didn't know her name, but I explained what she looked like and what she did as a job. I didn't hold out much hope of hearing from her again.

Liam, the kids and I went to the Cambridge Folk Festival a few days later. I'd bought the tickets long before I was diagnosed and was determined that we would still go. I felt slightly breathless on the journey, like a long-term smoker who needed to put their head out a window to gulp a mouthful of fresh air, but I put it down to being in a car with air conditioning.

The festival didn't disappoint. The bands and atmosphere were brilliant, and I swore I'd do it again the following year. We stayed in a hotel in Cambridge that night. I still felt very breathless but didn't say anything. It was easier to sleep once I was propped up on the pillows.

That night, whilst watching TV, an advert came on about holding a Macmillan coffee and cake morning. I took down the email address and decided there and then that I was going to hold one.

Lessons in womanhood – you are
only helpless when your nail polish is wet.
Even then you could
pull a trigger if you had to.

We awoke early the next morning with Liam roaring down the phone at one of his workers who'd not turned up at a job because he'd written down the incorrect postcode. Liam was like a lunatic and rushed us all out of bed to get home to sort it.

I still felt abnormally breathless so I texted my friend Claire, who is a nurse, to enquire about opening times and facilities in the walk-in centre. I thought all I needed was to find out my oxygen levels. Claire rang back and said I could go down anytime but it would probably be a long wait due to it being the weekend.

Liam was completely oblivious to my concerns. On the way back to Luton, I saw a sign for Stevenage and casually asked him to drive me to the hospital's A&E department as I'd had my surgery in that hospital.

Liam instantly looked panic-stricken and we were there in record time. I started to get very fearful, convinced that the cancer had now spread to my lungs, and I broke down numerous times. We didn't think we'd be there long because the receptionist told us they were unusually quiet.

I had to have bloods taken, but I was in such a state the nurse had to make several attempts.

Fiona kept texting me to find out how festival had gone and in the end I admitted that I was at the hospital undergoing tests but not to tell anyone.

Finally, I rang Donna at around 4pm; it wasn't fair on my kids being at the hospital since 9am and I wanted her to look after them. Donna was dumbstruck.

Liam dropped off the kids and came straight back. My mum kept texting me as I'd booked a hair appointment that day to get my hair cut shorter, and she wanted to go with me for moral support. I made excuses that I was caught up with something at Liam's work. In the end she rang Liam and he told her everything. She was deeply concerned.

The doctor told me that they needed arterial blood, which was quite painful to obtain as it needed to be taken from my wrist. I cried and cried whilst they were doing it.

At one point, I hummed the tune of 'Auld Lang Syne' – I've no idea why. The patients either side of the curtain must have thought I was under the influence of something pretty powerful.

Unfortunately, the arterial blood results were inconclusive as I was hyperventilating and they couldn't get a clear reading. The doctor declared that I would need a need a more detailed CT scan as they thought I might have a blood clot. I was sobbing uncontrollably, convinced I had lung cancer. I told Liam it was 'game over' if this was the case. I shouldn't have said that to him, but at that point I felt like I was just treading water.

Finally, after eleven hours, the nurse gave me some food. I hadn't been hungry until that point, which is unheard of for me. I was just about to start eating when the doctor came through and started reading the report.

He mentioned a pulmonary embolism and mentioned a four-millimetre nodule on my right lung and my spine. I pushed my food back and asked what the hell that was. He started to stutter then stammered that he didn't know.

I shouted, 'Has the cancer spread to my fecking lungs? I need to know! I need to know now!'

Shocked at my outburst, Liam begged me to calm down. Another doctor came through then and told me they were not experts at reading CT scans and could only treat me for the pulmonary embolism (blood clot).

He said I'd made the right decision in coming to A&E as some patients just keel over and die. Liam visibly paled at this point. On one hand I should have been pleased it was a blood clot, but on the other hand there was something suspicious that they didn't know about.

I was told that I would have heparin injections every day for six months as warfarin tablets could interfere with chemo. This was a major setback - I have a severe needle phobia. How the hell would I endure someone jabbing me for the next six months at the same time each day? Talk about throwing water on a drowning rat. The nurse injected me whilst I stood up and it hurt like hell, like a bee sting. I'm not the bravest patient, and I was beside myself thinking of what lay in front of me. In the midst of all this chaos, I got a text from the girl I'd met at Lister Hospital at the CT scan asking how I was doing. It turned out the receptionist at the CT department knew her and let her know I was asking for her. It was so lovely to hear from her – but at the same time I certainly wasn't feeling my best.

When I finally got home, my head was all over the place, exhausted and extremely emotional. Two of my friends visited and I cried my eyes out. My mum came round too and told me that my brother Kieran had come to her house and cried nonstop for forty-five minutes.

One of Liam's friends, who thought Kieran knew, had told him in the pub. Kieran is the silent type; although he is tall in stature, he crumbles at things like this. I told Mum that I wanted an alcoholic drink to calm me down and, bless her, she drove home and came back with some wine. I needed it and it tasted like manna from heaven.

Joanna, God love her, and her two friends came too after their day out in London which she'd cut short when she heard the news.

Joanna's eyes were red and swollen and I knew she too had been crying her eyes out.

The next morning, Liam was pissed off with me for drinking and hardly spoke to me. I felt guilty, but at the same time I felt justified.

He thought I'd compromised my breathing and he was not happy. He was adamant that we weren't going to Philomena's wedding in Ireland because I wasn't allowed to fly and I needed someone to inject me daily. I didn't say anything, but I knew that I had to go. I even thought about going to a vet daily or getting my friend Julie (who is also a nurse) to inject me.

The first few days I got my brother's girlfriend Michelle and my friend Claire (who are both nurses) to give me my injections. I remember thinking that this was nuts: I had six months of injections, 180 jabs, and I had to go and find someone to do them each time.

A few days later, Joanna, a few friends and I went to Studham for lunch. All my friends were drinking prosecco like it was going out of fashion.

I would have loved a glass but my breathing still felt laboured and I didn't want to do anything to compromise it. Joanna asked me discreetly how I was doing. I burst into tears and told her it felt like I was drowning, that I couldn't breathe properly. It was horrible to see her so helpless.

The girls all stayed out, but I needed to go home.

I went back in the evening to catch up with them and took my children and Liam. The other husbands came too. Everyone was well oiled by then.

I decided I would try to do my own injection, and I went into the toilet and psyched myself up. I couldn't even get the cap off the needle as my hands were shaking so much! This was crazy – I was a qualified veterinary nurse, and I couldn't even do that! My friend had to help me remove the cap and I went back into the toilet cubicle. I didn't put the injection in deep enough to start with and started injecting into my skin layer, which was very sore, and the injection began leaking out. I removed it and reinserted it, which was harder because the needle was blunt from my first failed attempt. I felt euphoric once I succeeded.

I was shaking like a leaf when I went back into the pub. I picked up my glass of Coke and was shaking so much that it dropped out of my hand and smashed into a million pieces on the floor. Liam ran over and I burst into tears. He was raging that I'd injected it myself because I was so traumatised and made me promise never to try to do it again. My poor children looked wide-eyed to see me shaking so much. That night, getting into bed, I noticed an enormous ugly purple bruise on my abdomen where I had injected wrongly and that really freaked me out.

Claire and Michelle injected me for the next few days until I could muster up the courage to try and do it myself. Michelle would often swing by after a busy day at A&E and inject me; nothing was ever too much trouble. My mum, God love her, offered to inject me too, but I knew that I would have to overcome my fear. Finally, I managed to do it at Mum's house, and I felt so proud even though I hated it. The trip to Ireland could go ahead!

Liam was still adamant that we weren't going. Frustrated, he announced that if I went to Ireland and died over there, they could toss me in the Irish Sea, and I could float home! Or better still, my sister Fiona could have me stuffed and put in her front room! It's a good job I don't take things to heart.

Donna made me laugh when she told me she'd been called into school as her son, my nephew Freddie, had punched another lad. Freddie, ever the quick thinker, had cashed in on me, his 'sick auntie', and reckoned he'd been fighting because he was so distraught about me. I think he swerved a punishment that day.

I needed to sort out my Macmillan coffee morning so I went onto the Luton Irish forum to organise a date. They were super helpful; nothing was too much trouble. I wanted to keep my mind busy and have something to aim for which could involve everyone and raise funds for cancer. We decided to hold it in September, a few weeks after my second chemo, when hopefully I'd be feeling a little less fragile. I was extremely excited about having something to focus on.

I made an appointment at my local hairdressers to get a short bob. I hoped this would give me an increased chance of keeping my hair during cold cap as I wouldn't have heavy hair pulling on my hair follicles. The hairdresser was quite surprised and asked why I was going for such a radical cut. I burst into tears and explained about my diagnosis.

I spoke at length to Yvonne the day before my chemo started and confided that I was sort of happy to get the first one under my belt and get on with it. She told me afterwards that when she came off the phone, she said to her husband James, 'That poor girl hasn't got a clue what lies ahead of her.'

Do what makes you happy,
be with those who make you smile,
and laugh as much as you can breathe.

I had so many positive messages from family and my friends. Claire thoughtfully gave me a box with everything in preparation of my chemo, including a digital thermometer, neck pillow, a CD and anti-ulcer sweets.

I didn't sleep well that night and tossed and turned continuously. I kept focusing on the ceiling in my bedroom, thinking that this time tomorrow I will have my first chemo, the first stage of getting those microscopic cancerous cells blasted out of my body.

Yvonne rang me again in the morning as her daughter-in-law had gone into labour. I remember her saying that we were both going on significantly different journeys that day, and I never felt so frightened in my entire life. Yvonne's daughter-in-law was bringing a new life into the world, and I was going to start fighting for mine.

When we arrived at the chemo ward, I was taken aback by how busy it was. Most people were probably sixty and over. I shouldn't have been here; I felt like I didn't belong to the 'chemo club' and I didn't want to be part of it. Even the word 'Macmillan' screamed cancer to me. I was like a rabbit caught in the headlights.

I looked at the other people's faces, trying see how ill they looked, to try and comprehend how they felt. I sat so close to Liam that I could have crawled into his pocket. I just wanted to be anywhere but there with my diseased body. I was twisted towards him, my legs facing him, and I had clasped my jacket shut to make myself as small as possible. Looking back now, it was a safety mechanism to stop this horrible experience from happening.

I was called through shortly afterwards. My knees felt like jelly, my heart was pounding, and I was shivering uncontrollably. A wonderful Polish nurse called me through to prepare my hair for the cold cap. The process involved freezing your hair follicles to about minus thirty-seven degrees so that you have less chance of losing your hair. It only works in four out of ten people, and most people still lose fifty percent of their hair anyway.

Liam was adamant that I shouldn't do this as it would cause extra trauma and take more time, but I was determined to give it a shot. Besides, I noticed that the cold caps were given from money donated by women who'd done the Moonwalk. I felt like I should try it as I'd been one of them a few months before .I also wanted to keep my hair so that people wouldn't know that I had cancer. As a friend once said, 'Nothing screams cancer louder than a bald head.' I wanted to look normal and not get any sympathy tilted pitying looks.

The nurse soaked my head with a spray bottle and covered my hair with conditioner. She explained that she was going to turn me into a 'frozen princess'.

I sat down and another nurse, Joseph, handed me a bucket of warm water. I was to place my hand in it because it would help to make my veins more prominent for the intravenous catheter.

I was shaking because of my acute fear of needles, and my hands were dripping with sweat. I kept the nuns' 'comforting cross' in my other hand throughout. Joseph kept asking me to calm down as I was crying uncontrollably. I looked around at the other women receiving chemo and they were laughing and joking with their nurses. I couldn't make eye contact with them.

I was given a concoction of tablets so that I wouldn't get sick. Once the intravenous catheter was in place, the cold cap was placed on my head and switched on. There was a chin strap which had to be pulled tight so that the hat was in complete contact with my head to ensure optimum results. I felt like the famous jockey, Frankie Detorri!

I've never felt cold like it – it took my breath away. Liam was trying to chat to me, but I couldn't speak for the pain.

Liam, God love him, even handed me his phone and told me to Google 'caravans' to try and distract me. I'd been thinking about buying one the previous week and Liam had refused; now he was actively trying to get me to pursue it. My eyes felt dead in my head. I felt like a dog on the vet's table that had come to the end of its life and was begging to be taken out of its misery and put to sleep.

After the first twenty minutes, the intense pain died down because my head was completely numb and frozen. Chemo could now commence.

Joseph had to sit with me whilst I received each bag, two clear ones and one bright red one. It was vital that I reported any pain to him as this would mean that the drugs had come out of the vein and it would not be good. I didn't look at any of the injections going into my veins because it would have unsettled me more. I had to get into my mindset that this was weed killer, killing those bastard weeds that had invaded my body.

I told Joseph that I was hoping to go to Ireland for a wedding. When he checked the dates, he said it would be unlikely that I could because I needed blood tests before my next chemo and it wouldn't fit in. I must have looked crestfallen because the next minute he came back and told me that I could get the blood tests done in a different ward the day before the chemo. Liam looked at me and said, 'I can't believe you've even managed to persuade the chemo unit to let you go to Ireland.'

I was freezing cold and the nurses had to keep putting extra blankets and more electric heat pads on me. I wished I'd been more organised like the South African woman opposite me who was also doing the cold cap; she was wearing wore a warm fleece and thick thermal socks. I had bloody sandals on! Liam took off his own socks and put them on my feet to try and warm me up.

The drugs were given slowly over a few hours. Once they were all in my system, the cold cap had to stay on another forty-five minutes.

After it was switched off, I still had to wait before I could remove it. My hair was frozen, so the hair would be pulled out from the root if I attempted to remove it before my head 'defrosted'. Once the cap was removed, I ran to the toilet as I was bursting for a wee. My urine was bright orangey-red like Lucozade from one of the chemo drugs. I was shocked to see it had gone through my system so quickly.

I was given steroids and numerous anti-sickness tablets to take home, along with immune-boosting injections that had to be injected into my abdomen on day four after the chemo and for the following seven days after.

I covered my fragile, frozen head with my baseball cap and headed to the car with Liam, shaky but relieved.

We went straight to my sister Donna's house where she had cooked dinner. I wolfed it down and even had seconds. My mum came round, anxious to see how I was.

I started to dip then and needed to go home. I felt weak and nauseous; if I'd been offered the same dinner again, I would have vomited. It was mad to think in such a small timeframe I could feel so bad.

I did manage to go and watch Orla at her Gaelic football training later that evening. I wanted to pretend that it was 'business as usual' and keep a sense of normality for my children.

Afterwards I went home to bed as I'd started to dip again. In the middle of the night, I was on my hands and knees trying to be sick in the toilet. The anti-sickness tablets prevented me vomiting, which seemed worse as I was sure I would feel better if I could be sick. I climbed back into bed, shaking uncontrollably and crying. I kept asking Liam how the hell I was going to do the rest of my chemo when I was feeling so bad and falling at the first hurdle?

I finally managed to wear Liam down and he agreed to go to the wedding in Ireland in a few weeks time. We were going on the ferry, which meant a long drive to Scotland as it sailed from Cairnryan to Belfast. Flying was out of the question due to my blood clot.

I hit a brick wall after the chemo and struggled hard to remain positive. I just couldn't stop crying; 'Tiny Tears' had made another unwelcome appearance and wasn't going anywhere. I had such black thoughts about dying and leaving everyone behind. I would sit in the armchair looking at the back garden, completely zapped of all my energy, staring at the trees and realising how beautiful nature was. Only now did I really appreciate it. I took long walks in the park with my beloved scruffy crossbreed, Dillon, to try and combat the feelings of utter despair.

All positivity had left me, and I was in a dark place. I stayed up later and later as I wanted to be exhausted when I went to bed. I didn't want to wake in the middle of the night because that was my most vulnerable and weakest time.

I often researched my cancer, even though I knew it was frowned upon. I was petrified by some of the negative posts in the cancer forums. Those dark thoughts of death loomed over me and I couldn't let that happen. I even texted my family and told them that I felt like I couldn't breathe with the constant bombardment of advice. They needed to refrain from talking about it. I felt suffocated being told what I should be eating, etc. Liam often told what I should and shouldn't be doing – more what I shouldn't be doing – and that made me more determined to rebel. I hate to be told what I can't do. I felt like a bird who'd had their wings clipped, a prisoner in my own body.

I got the number of a lady who did reiki sessions and went to see if she could do anything to help me stop feeling so utterly helpless.

She told me that there were lots of angels round me sending me healing, including St Anthony whom I have so much belief in. The reiki session was an hour long and for the first forty minutes I cried in the lady's arms. She was a stranger but I couldn't control my emotions.

I didn't think that I had the physical or mental strength to see the chemo through. I convinced myself that I would definitely go for a mastectomy once I had finished chemo because I would never go through this again. I wasn't ready to die; I had so much that I wanted to see and do. I had two gorgeous children that needed their mum now more than ever. But I still couldn't shift the black cloud that had engulfed me. It had swallowed me whole and was dragging me to the pits of despair.

On a night out with friends, I fell to my knees beforehand begging and pleading with God to help me, to get rid of this bastard that had taken up residence in my body. One evening whilst I was feeling particularly low, I reached out to the breast cancer support line and sobbed so much that I could hardly speak. I kept saying if only I had found the lump earlier. The lady simply said, 'Never look back, always look forward,' which is so true and became my mantra in life.

I was given a number to ring in the morning as the woman was so concerned about me. During it all, poor Ethan looked in through the half-open door at me; he looked frightened but he said nothing and simply closed the door.

In the morning, I rang the helpline and explained that I needed to speak to someone who'd gone through the same process as me – someone who had numerous affected lymph nodes and would need repeat surgery. It sounded like a young lad on the other end of the phone, and he was fantastic. He said he would make me his priority and get a lady who'd gone through a similar experience to ring that evening.

Later that night, I spoke at length to Pat. I don't even know if that was her real name. She was two years on and sounded so upbeat.

I was crying, asking her if I would ever wake up without thinking about cancer. She told me that she had made friends with four other women going through the same horrible process and they were all fine. All of them were living for the moment and not letting anything hold them back. She had always wanted to buy and do up an old property and she'd now done it. Another of her friends had always wanted to move to Spain and was currently living there. Pat had worn a wig because she didn't want people to see her with a bald head but on one occasion, feeling empowered, she bravely removed it as she was leaving hospital. Apparently, a woman in a car driving past roared at the top of her voice, 'Get some hair!' What a nasty piece of work and even worse from a woman to another woman walking out of a hospital door. That really angered me.

Pat spoke to me for forty-five minutes and not once did I feel like she was in a rush to get me off the phone. She was so uplifting; it was like a counselling and therapy session all rolled into one. I don't think she will ever understand the impact that phone call had on me.

Everything heals.
Your body heals. Your heart heals.
The mind heals. Wounds heal.
Your soul repairs itself.
Your happiness is going to come back.
Bad times don't last.

I decided that I would buy a wig in case I lost my hair despite the cold cap. I wanted everything in place because it was Sod's law that I'd lose my hair in Ireland the day of the wedding and I wouldn't be prepared.

I took Donna and Orla with me to the chemo unit to look at head scarves. I never even knew where that part of the hospital was, and now I was a regular visitor. I started bawling in the waiting room and one of the nurses took us into a side room. They kept asking what was wrong. Poor Orla looked terrified, but she said afterwards that she would wear a headscarf too if it made me feel better.

I explained that I couldn't bear having any more intravenous catheters; the thought of them was sending me crazy. I remember clasping my jacket closed again, as if it was my armour to protect myself.

I would have been a body-language expert's dream as I tried to protect myself from my cancer world.

Joseph, my previous chemo nurse, was called into the room. He gently explained that I would be an ideal candidate for a PICC line because people who were anxious or scared usually had nightmare veins.

The nurses were fantastic and reassuring but I still kept crying.

I was taken into another room to go through the head scarves with a lady called Marian. She was so upbeat; she was a volunteer and also a breast cancer survivor. She let me try on loads of head gear and finally I agreed on a grey headscarf. She also had Velcro fringes, which she tucked under my headscarf and Donna said how good it looked, though I thought I looked like a woman with a headscarf wearing a stick-on fringe. I was told that it couldn't be straightened as it would melt and to be especially careful opening an oven when wearing it! If I hadn't been crying, I would probably have laughed my head off at the thought – a posh new fringe melted to my forehead whilst I cooked a roast.

How the hell did it get to this? I declined the fringe as it just wasn't me. We went to Joanna's house and the four of us headed to a wig shop miles away.

A young lad was working in the shop and he guided me to a swivel chair. There was a poster in the shop saying 'No hair, don't care' which was anything but what I felt, and I started bawling again. He placed a wig on my head and turned me to face my audience. Orla, Joanna and Donna were saying yes or no to each hairpiece. I kept looking at my wigs and thinking how fake they looked; they were too perfect, didn't sit right on me and looked too 'wiggy', if there is such a word.

We finally agreed on one and the young lad clipped the fringe so it sat above my eyes. I purchased wig shampoo, spray and a special brush – more shite to add to my growing collection of cancer stuff. I wore my new synthetic hair out of the shop and felt so deflated. Donna and Joanna, God love them, kept telling me how great it was that I was wearing it so soon but I felt like the fight had gone out of me that day.

Whilst on a family shopping trip to a nearby village, we had lunch in the sunshine. I started to dip mentally as I took tablet after tablet to stop the sickness and steroids to make me feel better. It brought home to me how much medication I needed to take just for a simple day out. We went into a shop where my sisters made for the clothes section. I, with my cancer-tunnel vision, headed towards the headscarves. Then I had to run out of the shop as reality set in and I started to sob. My sisters came running out after me and tried to calm me down, but I'd had a moment of panic as I realised that my life would be so different and out of my control for the foreseeable future whilst I was under the doctors' care.

I started to get awful bone pain after the chemo; it felt like the bottom of my spine was being crushed, and I couldn't sleep properly. I spent my nights in a foetal position, but nothing stopped it. I remember going to town with the kids as Ethan needed jeans and I wanted to be there to help him choose them. I had to sit down in the shop because the pain was so bad. I also purchased Liam a pair of shoes as a surprise, but I was crying in pain during the five-minute wait to get the matching shoe. It seemed like eternity and I was so sore. I don't know what the assistant must have thought of me.

I kept wondering if the bone pain and the suspicious areas on the CT scan were linked; was I riddled with cancer? Ethan and Orla had to link arms with me as I hobbled round the shopping centre like an old-age pensioner.

I rang the chemo unit and they explained that the bone pain was probably due to the immune boosting injections which stimulate bone marrow. I was so happy to hear that and I took a coedemol that evening, which made a huge difference. I only take pain relief if I am in seriously bad pain. I wasn't being a martyr; I just figured that my liver was working hard to break down my chemo drugs without adding to its workload.

The day for departing to Ireland arrived and I struggled to feel excited. Normally I would have made umpteen lists of what to take – part of the fun is getting everything ready. But I wasn't feeling it at all.

I had to go to oncology that day and speak to the doctor about how I was after my first chemo. Liam couldn't make it as his phone was playing up and he was trying to get it fixed, so I took Orla. She stayed in the waiting room when I went in to see the doctor. She explained again about the CT findings and said she couldn't tell me what they were; I would have to wait till I was halfway thought my chemo regime before they would rescan me to see if there were any differences.

I kept asking her, 'Please can you tell me I am going to be okay?'

The doctor avoided the question, saying, 'We are doing everything we can for you.'

'Please,' I begged. 'Just tell me I'm going to be okay,' I repeated, but she wouldn't answer me.

I was crying my eyes out, so a Macmillan nurse was brought in to hold my hand and calm me down. Orla told me afterwards that she could hear my sobs from the waiting room. I was convinced that the doctor knew more than she was letting on and was telling me to enjoy my holiday as she thought the worst.

Orla and I went home to get ready for our journey. I packed the kids, dog, suitcases, wig, heparin injections and cancer paraphernalia into the car and set off. It was nuts the amount of stuff I needed since I was diagnosed; I'd never even taken as much as an Anadin before.

We stopped a few times on the way to the ferry in Scotland so that I could stretch my legs to prevent another clot and to use the toilet. After eight hours we arrived at Stena Line, only to be told that I had booked P&O. It wasn't a big deal as the P&O ferry was only another fifteen minutes up the road. The weird thing was that Liam kept getting texts from Stena Line, which we'd ignored.

Once we were on the boat, we settled down and I relaxed. However, that was short lived. I double-checked the texts on Liam's phone, only to realise that I had booked the return sailing via Stena line on the same date. That meant that we were meant to be in Belfast getting ready to go home!

Once I realised my error, I started shaking uncontrollably. Liam kept asking what was wrong. I ran to the reception desk and asked them for the Stena Line number, but they didn't have it. I Googled it on Orla's iPad and rang them to explain my massive mistake. The lady on the other end of the phone was awfully sweet and tried to book us on a return sailing for the day we wanted, but they were fully booked.

I was howling now and everyone on the ferry was looking at me. Liam kept telling me to calm down, but I was shaking. I was trying to explain to the woman that I had to have chemo and needed to be back in the UK, but there was no availability.

I rang Fiona, as I knew I would lose my signal once the ferry left the port. My poor sister couldn't make any sense of me as I was crying so much. Liam kept saying we wouldn't make the wedding now as we'd only be able to stay a few days and then go back. I had to be at that wedding; I had overcome so many obstacles to get there, and I didn't want to fail at the last minute.

By the time we arrived in Donegal, it was the very early hours. Liam and I were barely talking. It had been a long emotional day and I was so, so tired. I told Liam that I might never be back again as the CT scan probably meant the cancer had spread to my bones. He shouted at me to calm down and I headed up to bed. I woke up later, went down and curled up on the sofa. Liam was out walking Dillon.

He came back and we managed to sort out a sailing for the day after the wedding. It wasn't ideal, but at least we could still go and that was all I had ever wanted. It had become more than a wedding; it meant that I still had some control.

Fiona and the kids called later that morning as she lives less than an hour away in Dungiven. Fiona had a head cold so didn't dare kiss me, and we drove to the beach with the windows down as she didn't want me to get any of her germs.

When we arrived at the beach, I started sobbing. I told Fiona that I felt like I was walking through glue, I couldn't concentrate on anything and I was falling apart emotionally. The kids sensed my upset and lagged behind us. I was due to see a healing priest in a few days' time and I was hoping for a miracle that could lift me from this dark hole.

After Fiona left, Yvonne and her girls called round. She'd been worried sick as she couldn't get hold of me after my phone had died en route to Ireland, and she didn't know if we'd made it. I started to cry my eyes out and I ushered her upstairs.

Once upstairs I couldn't breathe and I felt myself going into full-scale panic attack.

Yvonne, normally a remarkably calm person, looked seriously concerned. She said, 'Michelle, maybe you need to see someone. I always said it's good to cry but this is clearly not normal. What is wrong? Tell me what is wrong.'

I said that I was going to die. Yvonne looked at me square in the face and said clear as day, 'Michelle, you are not going to die.'

I felt like a heavy burden had lifted from me. I can't explain it; I just felt such relief that someone had uttered those words to me. That was all I wanted to hear. With that simple sentence, Yvonne had done the job of any top therapist. I texted her later that night and thanked her. She told me afterwards that she was greatly concerned about me and that I had really scared her.

The evening before the wedding, Yvonne, Fiona and I headed off to Ramelton to see a healing priest, Father Sweeny. We attended his mass and he blessed us all afterwards. I was so thankful that they both came with me. I was willing to embrace anything at all. It did lift me a bit more, and I was beginning to look forward to the wedding the next day.

The best view comes from the hardest climb.

The day of the wedding came, and the weather was glorious. When Philomena came down the aisle looking radiant to the song 'I Will Be With You', I felt a golf-ball size lump in my throat. Orla looked up at me as if to say, 'please don't break down'.

It had been such an emotional few weeks and I was finally here. I'd done what I'd set out to do and it felt amazing, like I had climbed Everest. The wedding lived up to my expectations, and I was overwhelmed and honoured to be part of it.

Just before dinner, Yvonne rang to say there was another priest in Buncrana who wanted to see me and bless me. She'd been trying to get hold of him for ages and he had just contacted her. We left our dinner and sped off down the road to see him.

Father Carlin was a real gentleman. He placed his hand on my hand and Liam placed his hand on the shoulder of my affected side whilst Father Carlin prayed and blessed me. I was so grateful to both Yvonne and him for doing that.

I am not going bore you with each of my chemos, but I really struggled with every one of them. The trepidation the night before was the hardest because I could never sleep. The journeys there were nearly always in silence as I was

73

so emotional as I knew what lay in store. I felt like I was on my way to my executioner.

At my second chemo, I went to sit in my allotted place and just couldn't control myself. I turned round so not to get eye contact with all the other poor souls who were undergoing it. I always tried if possible to get a 'window seat' so that I wouldn't be on display to the other patients.

A white-haired elderly lady, who was also hooked up to the chemo drugs, tried to smile at me but I couldn't stop crying and had to turn my face away from her. I felt my whole body jolting as I cried with every cell in my body.

Joseph, my nurse, took me into a side room and kept saying, 'What's wrong? Please tell me.'

I told him that I hated being there, I hated the chemo and I hated the poison that was being pumped into my veins. He told me to take a few minutes to calm down, but I was adamant that I wanted to get on with the process so it would finish sooner. I didn't want to spend another unnecessary minute in the chemo ward.

He calmed me down and took me back to my seat. Liam looked at me and said, 'Jesus, what was all that about?'

When I told him what I'd told the nurse, he looked at me and said the nurse must have thought I was one spoilt bastard! Talk about tough love.

Every other person's partner in the chemo word was giving their partners reassuring words in soft tones and Liam was saying that to me. To be honest, it was exactly what I needed.

If Liam had changed tactic and been overly nice, that would have freaked me.

After my hair started falling out in handfuls, I decided to get it cut short in a pixie cut. It was depressing to see hair all over the bathroom, the pillow and sometimes even on my dinner plate. I rang the hairdresser's and they fitted me in and cut it extremely short. I kept a handful and they gave me an envelope to place it in. It was so strange to have such a short style after years of long hair, but I felt like I was back in control.

I put on a short-sleeved pink blouse and jeans and headed to school to pick up Orla, convinced that she would love my new look. She looked shell-shocked when she saw me and couldn't get me out of the playground quick enough.

She told me months later that she hated it; my short hairstyle and the PICC line made everything seem so real and she was petrified. She made me give the pink blouse to a charity shop; it represented her despair on that day. She said she'd gone to school that morning and everything had changed in the blink of an eye at the school pick up.

My crying became a bit of a private joke between Orla and me. She often said, 'Come on, Mum, you've nearly done a day without crying.' Of course that always changed, and we'd be back to square one again.

Orla was the one who would gently place a hand on my shoulder if I started to sob in the car. Ethan was different. He never confided in anyone apart from his sister; he never wanted anyone to pity him or treat him any differently.

He wanted to keep it all to himself, a massive undertaking for a mere fourteen year old.

Orla recalled one time the two of them were in a park when they saw a lady wearing a cancer survivor T-shirt.

Ethan told his sister, 'That will be our mum one day.' He looked out for Orla, who is four years his junior, and made me so proud to be his mum.

Chemos are hard on your whole body. Sickness, bone ache, sore mouth, extreme fatigue, blurry vision and constipation were just some of the side effects I faced each time. I likened it to being shot: you are hit hard and fast, then you stagger round with the bullet inside you until finally you get to your feet and start to feel better. Then you're shot again, this time with more bullets. My heart also felt sore, fatigued as if it were old and knackered and coming up to its expiry date. Many a time in the morning or middle of the night, I woke to Liam prodding me or staring at me to make sure I was still breathing!

I met a lot of people, mainly ladies, in the chemotherapy ward and I talked to more of them once I was at the halfway mark. I suppose I might have even appeared nosey as I asked loads of questions. There are always people who are worse than you, a cliché but a true one.

I met two ladies from Luton whom I really only knew before to say hello to. Jacqui and Margaret had also been diagnosed with breast cancer. We met for lunch and sometimes messaged each other with how we were feeling. I named us the 'Hair Bare Bunch', which seemed apt as we were all at various degrees of hair loss.

Looking back, it was quite comical meeting up for lunch. Jacqui was as bald as an egg; Margaret had a few strays one and I managed to keep a good bit of mine and did a strategic 'comb over'. I found it therapeutic to meet them; they understood what it was like to have chemo. Jacqui was incredibly strong and completely focused on the end result, but Margaret was more like me and struggled mentally with the whole process.

I found it so comforting to have friends who texted me to invite me out or see how I was feeling. Some just turned up and sat with me. I always made sure I texted them back, as they'd taken time out of their day to see how I was. I had so many flowers delivered, holy relics given, prayers offered, dinners made, and masses said. I was blown away with people's kindness.

One of my retired neighbours, Yvonne, texted me every morning to see how I was. Even when her son died prematurely due to an undiagnosed heart condition, she still texted me – and she still does today. Collette's mum, Pauline, baked me Irish treacle and soda bread as sometimes this was the only thing I could face during chemo. I often returned home from a hospital trip to find her freshly baked goods tied to my front-door handle.

Another time, when my friends knew I wasn't up to going out for lunch, they brought lunch to me, and we had a great time putting the world to rights. I got beautiful inscribed jewellery, holy candles, and bottles of red wine (as Mum said it was better for me), quote pictures and so many texts that I could write another book about them. I once got an egg cup delivered from a friend, Claudia, as I'd made a passing comment that Liam would only allow me to drink small amounts of alcohol from an egg cup.

Julie in Ireland, and another particularly close friend Louise, set up a buddies' group to text me to see how I was doing. Carol, another friend, had every chemo, surgery and radiography session marked off in her head and never failed to send me a card, flowers or words of encouragement.

Fiona managed to track down a Padre Peo glove in London. This is a holy relic that has great healing properties and is sometimes associated with miracles. Padre Peo was a saint who had scars on his hands that corresponded to the wounds that Jesus sustained at his crucifixion. Some people who had touched or been blessed by the glove swore that they had been cured. I'm not a 'holier than thou' person by any stretch of the imagination, but I was willing to try anything.

Liam, the kids and I went to Victoria Station and found this little bookshop tucked away. I was blessed by the glove and we went into the basement to pray for about two hours. Ethan and Orla kept looking at me as if to say, 'Is this prayer session ever going to end?' It wasn't quite the day out in London that they'd envisioned.

At one point in my treatment, I located a faith healer in Ireland. He was a seventh son of a seventh son which in Irish folklore was a very lucky omen and he was considered to possess healing powers. He was a wild, curly-haired man of about seventy years old. I emailed him to say I would pay for him to fly over and put him up in my house, but he never responded. I didn't tell Liam; I thought I would cross that bridge when I picked up the healer from the airport. I think I'd have had an awful lot of explaining to do if he had flown over.

Mum agreed to move in with us each time I had chemo because I wanted the children to have as little upheaval in their lives as possible. I felt it gave her a real purpose, too; she wanted to be there to help in any way she could. A home-cooked meal is something we take for granted, but I just didn't have the energy to do it.

Ethan, Orla and Liam were delighted to have Mum there. She'd arrive with a ginormous shopping bag. She made me laugh because she scoured the internet for cures and tried to pump them into me. There was no such thing as half measures! Nuts, bicarbonate of soda, green tea, pomegranate, seeds, manuka honey – she purchased jars of honey for about £50 quid and went mental if I didn't take it every day. She also made up recipes in her nutribullets for me to drink, so packed with vitamins and fruit that they were no longer liquid, and you needed a fork to eat them!

My saucepans were binned; Mum deemed them unsafe as they weren't one hundred percent stainless steel. Even my deodorant was disposed of as it contained aluminium, and she thought this was carcinogenic. Mum recalled my fruit-picking days in Australia many moons earlier as cancerous due to the crops being sprayed with pesticides.

Claire had bought me a book with recipes for people going through cancer. She covered the word itself with some fabric so that we wouldn't see it. Mum, God love her, spent nearly two hours trying to get ingredients for some of the concoctions. She drove the supermarket assistants crazy searching for far-flung ingredients that she couldn't even pronounce.

Mum was always coming round with newspaper cuttings about new and wonderful 'cures'. I also trawled the internet to see if there were any advances in curing cancer. So many sites reckoned that chemo and radiation were bad for your body and should be avoided, but I wasn't planning to turn down any medical advice or treatment that was in my care plan. Each to their own. I did find it uplifting to hear about people who had come out the other side after cancer. It was the one thing that really lifted me when I was going through chemotherapy.

Dad always asked me the same questions: are you eating well and are you sleeping well? Bless him, he thought that was the cure for everything. Sometimes he would forget himself and tell me about someone who had recently died. When I asked what from, he'd tell me cancer and I would fall apart. God love him, he was so hell-bent on not mentioning about people with the C word that he said it all the time. In the end I told him that I couldn't be listening to negative stories because I wasn't mentally strong enough to deal with them. I wanted to hear the stories about people who had survived and were living life to the full.

We had a family WhatsApp group, which was ideal as I could let everyone know in one hit how I was feeling and if I was up for visitors.

My youngest sister, Joanna, was incredibly excited when her daughter, Isla Rose, was invited to her first Disney-themed 'Frozen' party. I'd just come out of the bath when Joanna called round. I was losing clumps of my hair, despite the cold cap. When I combed it, it was like dreadlocks falling out. I was extremely distressed by this and I was bawling. Joanna was shocked when she saw the amount of hair loss. Instantly, she cancelled going to the party that she'd been so looking forward to and stayed with me. I really wanted her to go but she said, 'I want to stay with you. There will be other parties.'

Another thing that stands out was that I had a real phobia of needles and my family arranged for me to see a hypnotist three times. I think it helped me a little, though I am by no means 'cured' as I still don't like intravenous injections or blood being taken. When I went to pay the hypnotist (which was not cheap), he told me that my family had paid for me.

My aunt and some of my cousins clubbed together and gave money to my sister Fiona in Ireland to pay for her to fly over and back to see me whilst I was ill. My other cousin wrote to the Pope and I had blessed rosary beads sent back to me.

Fiona told me that one time I had freaked her out. She rang me to see how I was after one of my chemos and I sounded so drained it was like I was a zombie. She came off the phone distraught; she thought the chemo was sucking away my personality. She later confided that she felt like she'd been talking to a stranger. Fiona sent me photos of robins and rainbows; we both took those as really good omens.

I took myself to the nuns a few times to pray in their garden when they were out visiting people. I attended their healing mass for the sick, which was packed, and we were all anointed. Sister Kathleen and Sister Antoinette became extremely good friends of mine.

Sometimes it takes balls to be a woman.

I had to attend hospital to have a PICC line fitted because of my needle phobia. This would make it much easier to take my pre- chemo blood tests before each session, and I could also receive chemotherapy through it.

I was so scared having it inserted because it is classed as a surgical procedure, and I was bawling by the time I reached the reception desk. The nurse who was going to do the procedure explained everything in detail and again I felt myself tightening my denim jacket as if to block it out.

Another nurse held my hand whilst it was being done. I was told to breathe in through my nose and out through my mouth during the procedure, which helped enormously. I didn't look at my arm the whole time, nor at the PICC line that would be going into my vein. I was X-rayed to make sure it was in place.

In hindsight, I wish I'd had the PICC line fitted before I started my chemotherapy as my veins were badly affected by the first two chemos. They felt unusually tight, as if they'd been burned or injected with something caustic – which I suppose they had been. I had to make weekly visits to the QE2 Hospital to have the line changed and flushed. They were so good there; I would avert my eyes as they did it then covered it up with a piece of bandage tubing. I am so squeamish when it comes to things like that, so it was better not to see it. Later I made my own tubing with a sock to match my outfits if I was going out somewhere.

I held my Macmillan coffee morning after my second chemotherapy. I loved having something else to focus on, apart from the C word. I advertised via Facebook and asked for people with obvious illnesses, including coughs and colds, to stay away as I didn't want to compromise my already diminished immune system. I was blown away by the number of people who came, helped, made cakes and donated.

I was exceptionally tearful in the lead up to the day; I was losing lots of hair and I thought I might be bald by the time it arrived. I decided that I needed my hair cut a lot shorter as it would seem less traumatic seeing shorter hair on the pillow and in the bath than clumps. Liam said, 'Well if you're bald and anyone finds a hair in their cakes, at least it won't be yours!'

The Irish forum was buzzing – it was such a vibrant atmosphere. I did get a slight knock back as a friend told me that Jackie Collins, the famous novelist, had died from breast cancer that very day. I couldn't dwell on it, though, as the donations of cakes and money kept coming and we were rushed off our feet.

We had a shock visitor that day in Daniel O'Donnell, the Irish singing sensation. My friend Beatrice knows him as she is a neighbour of his from Donegal. This was all arranged secretly because he was appearing in Strictly Come Dancing.

Liam got the phone call about an hour before to collect Daniel from the train station in his Ford pick-up. It still makes me laugh; he told me afterwards that one of his friends asked him why he was leaving the Irish forum and he said, 'I'm on my way to pick up Daniel O'Donnell.' As he reversed the pick-up out of the car park, his friend was still scratching his head.

It was a wonderful surprise and Daniel was a true gentleman. He explained how awful his wife Magella had felt when she went through breast cancer. People were taking out their phones and getting selfies with him. He seemed genuinely concerned about the treatment; I felt he was such a sincere, kind-hearted man.

Two of the local pubs, O'Sheas and The Phoenix, were so charitable too. I had a large sum of money donated from one, and the other supplied all the teas and coffees. The people of Luton were generous and kind, and I felt truly humbled by the people of my town.

I was contacted by Macmillan afterwards who told me that my coffee morning was one of the most successful in the UK – we raised more than £5,200!

Fiona and Philomena did the Lough Derg pilgrimage, which involved a lot of walking and praying. They held a Macmillan coffee morning the week after and raised lots of money. My friend Wendy told me that she had attended a group psychic meeting a few days earlier to see if any family members might 'come through'. The psychic told her he could see a woman with a wig, which was uncanny as I'd modelled the wig to Wendy a few days earlier. He went on to tell her, 'Don't be worrying about your friend. She's going to be okay.' I'm normally a bit sceptical about psychics, but it gave me such a lift to hear that.

A few days after my halfway mark with chemo, my dad and I went to bank the money. We decided not to use my local branch in Luton because it was always so busy and drove to a quieter branch a few miles from my home. When I gave the money to the bank clerk, he said he couldn't accept it in the form it was in as it was all in change with the exception of a few notes.

The manager came out and handed Dad and I a handful of money bags and said it must be counted out before he could accept it. I explained that it was for money raised by a Macmillan cancer coffee morning, but that didn't make any difference.

Dad and I sat down in the empty bank and started the long drawn-out process of counting out the money. Not once did the clerk or the manger come out to help us. The only person who came into the bank was the Securicor man to pick up money, so it wasn't as if they were busy. We sat for at least forty minutes counting the coins, putting them into piles and then placing them into bags. I felt so nauseous from the smell of the money that I thought I'd throw up.

I handed the manager the money. He pushed numerous money bags across the table to me and said they weren't counted properly and he wouldn't bank them till they were. I started to cry and said that not once did they offer to help us. I felt more and more faint and sick.

I didn't mention the fact that I had cancer and had just undergone chemo. My poor dad didn't know what to do. The manager had a complete lack of understanding or compassion and I left in tears with bags and bags of loose coins. I spoke to my sister about it; unbeknown to me, she rang the bank and told them how awful they'd made me feel from something so good. The manager said to Fiona that I should have mentioned that I was going through treatment, but why should I have? That was the only negative thing I experienced whilst I went through my treatment plan.

After a visit to Dr Crawley, he decided that I would need another lumpectomy instead of a mastectomy and it was scheduled for 17th December. I was surprised; I had my head round to thinking about a mastectomy but he was adamant that was all I needed, so who was I to argue?

For the first time, Liam and I left the hospital smiling. We felt relieved that the operation was not going to be so hard on me, and it was a lot simpler than a mastectomy. It would all be done and dusted by Christmas. Mum was apprehensive about a lumpectomy, but I told her that the doctor had insisted it would be fine. And who were we to argue with the experts?

All the best things are wild and free.

I had to undergo another CT scan on the 2nd of November to check the two areas which the doctor was previously unsure about. I was petrified because this would show whether they had increased, which would not be a good sign. If they had disappeared, it meant they had been cancerous and had been zapped by the chemo. The best outcome would be that they were still the same size; this would mean that they were possibly previous injuries or lesions that were non-cancerous.

I attended the nuns' house the day before my results and Liam, Ethan, Orla and I said a little prayer in the garden.

This lingering feeling of the unknown had hung in the air for three long months; I couldn't move forward until I knew. I even stopped writing this book because I couldn't go any further without knowing I was going to be okay.

Liam and I went to the hospital to see the oncologist. We went in through a different entrance, as if this could be a sign of good luck. My doctor finally uttered the words that I'd so wanted to hear for the last twelve weeks: the areas on the CT scan had remained the same size. I could have hugged him. I kept asking him to repeat it, as I still couldn't believe it.

I made sure we left by the same door and ensured I went through my same 'lucky' entrance after that. I still do, each time I go to hospital. I met my friends for lunch and we were all on cloud nine. My family was over the moon, my mum's novenas had been answered and finally we had some happy news.

My friend Julie's mum, Rose, was admitted to hospital just before my fifth chemo. She sounded very poorly and it was so sudden, but I thought she would be fine. Julie flew over from Ireland to be with her. She texted me to say that things were not looking good.

Claire and I went to visit Rose, and I was astounded at how ill she looked. She was heavily sedated and had tubes everywhere but I was still convinced that she'd pull through as she was as fit as a fiddle before. We left the hospital around 11.30pm. Julie and her brother were called back a short time later. Rose had passed away. That knocked them, and us, for six. Rose had been perfectly fine but had ended up with a kidney infection which subsequently led to septicaemia and kidney failure.

Poor Julie was in bits and I felt awful leaving her, but I had to be at the hospital for my fifth chemo. This was the only time that I did not cry on the journey there. I felt so sad for Julie and her brother who would be viewing Rose's body when I was going through chemo. It put things into perspective.

The nurse attached the cold cap to my head, but I was in a trance so I didn't push it down to fit properly – I lost most of my hair after that.

I also ended up with thrombo-phlebitis a few days later and had to be hospitalised with intravenous antibiotics for four days. I was determined that I would be out in time for Rose's funeral. She always said she wanted a celebration of her life if she was ever to die, and that is what she got! It was one of the best send-offs a person could have hoped for, surrounded by friends and family.

There were tears but lots of laughter, drink and dancing. I drank copious amounts of red wine and don't remember getting home that night. I woke up the next morning still in my funeral clothes!

I started having to colour in the top of my scalp with a brown pen because of the hair loss. I would gently blow dry my hair over the big bald area in the centre. I used to think it was funny to see bald men with comb overs and now I was one of them. I sent a picture to my family, and they were pretty stunned by it. To be honest, the stuff I used to cover it was my saving grace because it covered my white scalp well.

One time when I went to visit Liam, he took one look at me and said, 'You need to start wearing a scarf or bandana as it is incredibly noticeable.' I thought he was exaggerating until I caught sight of myself on the CCTV in the yard; it looked like I was wearing a white skull cap.

I lost every eyelash, too; this alarmed me as it felt like I was losing my femininity. My eyes felt constantly itchy where the eyelashes had fallen in and were now rubbing the eyeball. I'd get out the mascara and then realise there was not one eyelash for it to go on. I looked at women with long hair and eyelashes and felt so envious.

It always seems impossible until it is done.

The day of my final chemo arrived. I was willing it be over. It was November 25th – exactly one month before Christmas. I had overdosed on all my Christmas decorations as I was so looking forward to not having to worry about more chemo. I had every decoration that you could think of, from a reindeer duvet cover to robin tea towels. I'd even bought two massive light up garden reindeers, and squashed them into the back of my Fiat 500 with the seats down and the boot half open. My friends often turned up with Christmas memorabilia as they knew how much we, as a family, were looking forward to it.

Early that morning I felt my stomach gurgling and making strange sounds. I started to feel sick but pushed it to the back of my mind. Everyone was texting me to wish me the best of luck and say well done, it was all going to be over soon. I tried to ignore the pain in my stomach but then I went to the toilet and started vomiting. This couldn't be happening today of all days.

Liam rang me from work to see what time we were going, and I told him that I couldn't leave the toilet. Not only was I throwing up, I also had profuse diarrhoea. I rang the chemo ward and had to keep stopping speaking so that I could vomit. I contemplated asking them if they could hook me up to the chemo drugs in the disabled loo as I was so determined that it would still go ahead. Did it have a plug socket to plug my cold cap into? Throughout all my chemo I'd been so focused on November 25th being my final date; it was the light at the end of a tunnel.

The nurse said I'd have to cancel my appointment, but I should be able to come in on Friday instead. Fiona was flying over from Ireland the following week and we had a surprise fortieth party booked for her, so I was adamant that Friday would be the day. However, a short time later the senior chemo nurse rang to inform me, in no uncertain terms, that my chemo would not be until the following Thursday.

I was crying my eyes out and could hardly speak between sobs. I kept saying that my sister was coming over from Ireland and we were having a party for her that had been arranged around this final chemo. The nurse was extremely blunt and told me that if I underwent chemo whilst not one hundred percent fighting fit, I could end up in intensive care.

All I could think about was that I was going to be drained for the party and for all the people who were going to be there, including Yvonne and James. I lay on the sofa so despondent, feeling like the wind had come out of my sails.

My dad came to visit me, but I kept crying. I had to ring the Lister Hospital where I was to have my lumpectomy and explain about the week's delay because I knew this would have a knock-on effect and put my surgery back. A short time later, Dr Crawley rang. After discussing me in an oncology meeting, they had decided that a mastectomy was the only answer to try and prevent the cancer from returning. I felt like I'd been shot from every angle.

Wednesday, 25th November 2015, was not a good day for me.

Ethan, bless him, tried to lift my mood by saying that we could at least put up the Christmas decorations at the weekend when I'd be in good form and wouldn't be feeling sick. It was the kick up the arse I needed. I was still gutted about the delay, but I could see the reasons for it. The nurse did ring me back and managed to get the chemo session one day earlier, so that was some improvement.

Two days later, I made my weekly visit to the QE2 Hospital to have my PICC line dressed and flushed. I was so upset that I could feel myself welling up when the nurses asked how I was. I went into a nearby shopping centre to try and cheer myself up and get a few Christmas presents.

Whilst I was in the queue with presents for my niece and nephew in Ireland, a Christmas carol came over the speaker, 'So This Is Christmas' by John Lennon. It hit me so hard, I felt I'd been punched in the stomach. Christmas was coming and I still needed one more chemo. I felt a tennis-size ball in my throat and I couldn't control myself – I was in a long queue, crying my eyes out.

I purchased my items and made my way to the lift to the car park. It was packed but I backed into a corner and sobbed. I did get a few funny looks in the lift but most people stared ahead, ignoring the cry baby.

I got into my car and at that point Fiona rang me.

I was in a bad way and she felt powerless to help me. In hindsight, I should have gone home straight after having my PICC line flushed, but I was so deflated when they put my chemotherapy back. I know it was only seven days, but a week is an awfully long time when you are going through chemo.

I recovered after my final chemo much quicker than any of the others, probably due to mind over matter. I knew that (hopefully) I wouldn't be coming back in to be hooked up to poisons, and I wouldn't be zonked out by all the side effects. I even managed to do a side kick as I was leaving the hospital. I was so happy to be seeing the back of the chemo ward!

Fiona came over for her fortieth and, although I was only two days post-chemo, I was in mighty form. Nothing was going to stop me enjoying myself. I ate lots, drank lots, and was evidently merry. This continued all over Christmas and New Year. Nothing and nobody was going to get me down.

On Christmas Day, my family had clubbed together and got me a day at the spa, which was such a thoughtful gesture. On Boxing Day, we were all at Donna's house having a bite to eat and I was on the phone to Fiona when she walked in the door!! It was a big surprise that she had booked to come over too for the spa day.

I was very anxious as my impending surgery date got nearer, the 25th of January. I saw the doctor, Miss Darcy, who was going to do it and she explained what was going to happen in detail. She was like a breath of fresh air. I had an immediate rapport with her; she was so kind, and I felt that I really mattered to her. She was adamant that, as well as being cancer free, my cosmetic outcome would be good. I was to undergo a mastectomy with an immediate temporary reconstruction with an expander implant. It was hard to take in that I was going to lose my breast.

Miss Darcy was exceptionally compassionate. She said that it is so hard on a woman to be faced with this decision, and she respected that it wasn't to be taken lightly. I did get tearful when I thought about it, but I knew there was no way round it.

After I'd had my initial surgery to remove the lump, I looked at my breast differently. It is hard to explain but it felt alien to me, and I felt let down for what it had harboured inside. I wouldn't touch it and could barely look at it. I can only liken it to a friend who had turned against me, and I would be better off without. I was reminded of it every time I undressed and saw the scar. I had to get into that frame of mind because this was my coping mechanism for having my breast removed.

I went out with friends the weekend before the surgery, but I was an emotional wreck and I broke down in bits when they played my song 'Wake Me Up When It's All Over'. It seemed even more significant now.

Keep smiling because life is a beautiful thing and there's so much to smile about

The day of my surgery came. I'd been told that I would probably be operated on around 11am. I handed Orla my special necklace with all my holy medals on it. She wanted to wear it and told me that she'd clasp it if she missed me so she could feel close to me.

I arrived at the hospital at 8am to go through the forms. My doctor greeted me wearing her scrubs and introduced me to her all-girl anaesthetist team. She said they were going to really look after me. They were sweet, but I was so tearful.

The registrar asked if I wanted some additional drugs to calm me down. It was not part of the protocol, but they'd give them to me if I needed them. I said that I didn't want anything extra in my body if it wasn't required. I also refused to have a urinary catheter fitted. Dr Darcy said that I'd probably be in pain post-surgery and might not be able to make the bedpan, but I told her stubbornly that I would make it.

We had a long wait and weren't called until after 2pm. It all happened extremely fast then, and I had to say goodbye to Liam, who hadn't left my side since we'd arrived. I burst into tears and hugged him. There were tears in his eyes as I was led off to theatre; those were hard to see.

When I awoke from surgery, I was so relieved that it was over. My affected breast was now on its way to the laboratory to make sure it was all clear. The nurse rang Liam; she told me that he'd said that he loved me very much, and I asked her to say the same back to him. 'Please stop it,' she said. 'You'll have me in tears in a minute.'

I was transferred to a ward with three other ladies, where I recovered for the next seven days. I had a big drain coming out of the op site and had to be careful when moving in bed. I also had IV morphine and a machine to massage my legs to minimise the risk of another blood clot.

I looked away when the nurses and doctors checked my wound as I couldn't bring myself to look at it. I just wasn't ready. I couldn't even change into my own nightwear because the thought of looking at my wound made me feel shivery, so I stayed in the hospital gown.

My surgery involved an implant like an orange. Half of it was silicone gel and the other half was empty. I had a port under the skin; gradually, over the next few weeks, I would have fluid injected into it to stretch the skin and make the breast more symmetrical.

Miss Darcy came to see me one day after the operation. I was so in awe of her dropping by to see me that I burst into tears. It made me feel like I wasn't just a number but that I mattered to her. In all fairness, she always made me feel like I was important to her, and I will be forever grateful for that. I can't praise her enough; her surgery was flawless, and I was thrilled to see that the new part of my body was so well done.

I wanted to go to a friend's engagement party that weekend, but it wasn't meant to be. My drain had to stay in longer as there was still a lot of fluid being drained from my body. I think my mum and Liam were secretly delighted – they thought I was nuts to even consider going.

One of the trainee doctors came to see me shortly after my surgery, and I asked her if the breast which was removed seemed to be clear. She said that there was a lump there. I found that odd, but I didn't question it. The next day, when she came to check me again, I said that surely my lump would no longer be there after the surgery and the chemo. She apologised and told me she'd mixed me up with another lady. I found this peculiar, and I thought she was saying that so as not to worry me until I got my results.

The Macmillan nurse also came to check on me. She mentioned that sometimes the breast tissue might still contain some cancer despite the harsh treatment it had received; if that was the case, I would just need to be 'zapped' with chemo again. I really thought they were preparing me for the worst. When I mentioned it to my mum, she questioned me at length and I knew she also thought it wasn't going to be favourable news.

One lady I met on the ward was only in for one day. She was very spiritual, and she told me that she could see angels and people's auras. When I asked her what colour aura I had, she said it was white, which meant that there were lots of healing angels around me. I was extremely happy with that.

The day after she left, I Googled white auras and saw that in some cases it meant death. That scared the hell out of me. I even tried to remember the lady's name so that I could message her and see if she was telling me the truth. Irrational behaviour, I know, but that is how I was.

I met some truly inspirational ladies on the ward and have kept in contact with some of them. They also struggled with the dreaded C word. The fact that we were all getting treatment was a good omen. I got Liam to treat them all to a MacDonald's one dinner time; they were so appreciative and we felt like queens eating it in our ward.

The hospital Catholic layperson popped in to visit me. She was sweet; she drew the curtains around my bed and made a simple altar on my table and we prayed together.

I walked every day, especially around three or four in the morning when I couldn't sleep. I walked round and round the ward, determined not to get another blood clot. I also kept my surgical socks on another seven days after I got home as I was not willing to take any more risks.

I was finally discharged and delighted to return to the comfort of my own home. About a week or so after the surgery, I got the news that I'd been hoping for: there was no cancer in the breast that they had sent away. I kept asking the doctor to repeat it and I even got her to photocopy the lab report so I could see it for myself and read it repeatedly. Even though half of it was medical jargon that I couldn't understand, I wanted a hard copy in my hands.

Every few weeks I went to see Miss Darcy at the QE2 Hospital and she injected saline into the port at the side of my breast to make it more symmetrical. She would try and slightly overinflate it, as she knew of my needle phobia and wanted to cut down the number of hospital visits.

One day, after she put about 200mls in, I could hardly drive home. The pain was unreal; I took morphine and it didn't even touch it. I had to sleep in another room for a few days because I hit the ceiling if Liam accidentally rolled near me on the bed. I slept propped up on about eight pillows and couldn't move from that position. Getting from lying down to standing up was unbelievably painful.

I attended Mount Vernon Hospital shortly afterwards to get markers for my radiotherapy, which was next in my treatment programme. Unfortunately, it couldn't go ahead; I couldn't let any of the staff touch me because I was in agony, and I was sent back home.

After about five days, the pain subsided enough for me get my markers at Mount Vernon. This involved numerous X-rays and scans of my chest area, measurements being taken and numbers shouted out by the radio team which meant absolutely nothing to me. I had three dots permanently tattooed on me that they could use as markers for my radiotherapy. Unfortunately, they found that my heart was directly 'in the line of fire' for the radio beam. I would have to learn to hold my breath for at least twenty seconds when the radiotherapy was being used on certain areas to stop it hitting my heart.

The breathing exercises were due on the 18th of March in the morning. This was not ideal as it was St Patrick's night the day before. Liam and I had gone out and given ourselves a curfew but we kept changing it as the craic was so good. We drank to the early hours, so I was intensely hungover when I got to the hospital. I apologised to the radiographer and his team for the smell of alcohol. They laughed and said they were only jealous that they hadn't been out with me. I managed to hold my breath so well that day that the radiographer recommended that I got drunk before each session!

Before radiotherapy started, the nurses were suspicious that I might have another blood clot because I was notably breathless walking up the stairs. They did a blood test, which strongly indicated that this might be the case. This was a major setback.

I went to the Lister Hospital with Michelle, my brother's girlfriend. The doctor struggled to get a vein and even used an ultrasound to try and find one. It was a nightmare, but she finally got one inside my wrist. She explained that if I had a blood clot, I would need to be on medication for the rest of my life. That just floored me.

Halfway through having my scan done, it had to be halted. The cannula was not attached properly, and it squirted everywhere.

They hooked me up again, and this time I felt a horrendous pain shooting up my wrist. The CT scan had to be cancelled because I had 'tissued'; the IV cannula was no longer in the vein and dye was leaking into all my surrounding tissue.

My wrist had swollen and it was so painful. The nursing team kept putting bags of ice to try and alleviate the swelling. I was in a terrible state and sobbing uncontrollably, so they let Michelle in to see me. She was brilliant and managed to calm me down and slow my breathing.

They decided to do the CT scan through the PICC line; initially they'd thought that enough dye couldn't be injected through it to be diagnostic. Eventually they told me they had a diagnosis, and I would have to wait to see the doctor.

I was called into his room a short time later and he explained that he could not see a blood clot, nor could he see any cancer. I skipped out of his room like a teenager.

*Look for something positive in each day,
even if some days you have to look a little
harder.*

I needed eighteen sessions of radiotherapy, so we were unable to go to Ireland for Easter as we'd hoped. We went to the hospital five days a week at different times, and the radiotherapy took twenty minutes each time. Holding my breath was hard and I felt such relief when they told me that I could breathe normally after the countdown.

Radiotherapy was a walk in the park compared to chemo, although two weeks after it finished I did get seriously burned. My armpit was red raw and the skin went black. When I had a bath, the skin fell away like a snake's. I used a special cream from the doctor and it made a big difference. I was unusually red on my breast and on my back where the radiotherapy beam had exited.

I was prescribed a daily tablet, anastrozole, and had monthly implants to try and eliminate any oestrogen in my body. My tumour had been oestrogen fed, so it was vital that my ovaries closed down. My body had been more or less pushed into early menopause after my second chemo. The tablets made me experience awful night sweats; I often woke up with my nightwear soaked through. I was forever pushing the blankets off in the night, only to pull them back on five minutes later as I was freezing again. The tablets needed to be taken once daily for ten years so I hoped that my body would adjust to them in time.

I joined a slimming group as my weight had steadily increased with the medication and the steroids. Donna thought I was mad trying to focus on losing weight along with my treatment, but I wanted to be back in the driver's seat and start taking control of how I looked. I had thought that cancer would make me lose weight, but the opposite was true. I found out afterwards through my oncologist and research that cancer thrives in fat cells, so I was going to try my best to reduce its chance of rearing its ugly head again. I wanted to start feeling like me and be in control of my destiny.

I kept my PICC line in because I wanted it for my final surgery. I was also trying to get the BRCA test done to determine if I carried the faulty gene and therefore my daughter and sisters would be at more risk of cancer. So far I'd been refused BRCA testing by the NHS, but my friend Claire was appealing on my behalf.

Even though Miss Darcy's reconstructive surgery was brilliant, it was only temporary. I had to decide what permanent route of reconstruction I wanted. I decided against the silicon implant because I thought it would look fake against my natural breast and opted for surgery, which involved taking fat from the lower abdomen and transferring it to make a breast. It was a much more natural approach as it would be my own tissue and not a foreign object being put into my body. With a minimum six-month post-radiation wait, hopefully my body wouldn't reject it. Radiotherapy can affect the blood vessels and it could ruin the one chance of surgery I had if I underwent the huge, complicated procedure too soon.

Life might not have been the party
that we had hoped for
but whilst we are here,
we may as well dance

The PICC line needed to be redressed and flushed every week at the QE2 Hospital. Although this was a pain, the staff were super- efficient and I never had too long to wait. On one of my weekly visits the PICC line felt itchy and sore twenty-four hours after being flushed. Typically, it was on the day that a group of friends, Liam and I were going to Birmingham for two nights to see the Dixie Chicks. The break had been booked for about ten months and we were so excited about it, but I decided to go back to hospital to have the PICC checked. Something definitely was not right.

The nurse said it looked extremely inflamed at the point of entry and recommended removing it. I begged her to reconsider; I needed it because my needle phobia. I asked her for antibiotics instead. She brought the doctor, who gloved up and examined me. Before I knew what she was doing she said, 'It's got to go,' and pulled it out of my arm. Apparently, there was a golf-ball sized swelling tracking up my arm. She explained that the PICC line was acting like a train track and the infection was gradually working its way up my arm towards my heart.

I was given very strong antibiotics, but I was unbelievably crushed and I cried my eyes out all the way home. We still went to Birmingham, though, and we had a brilliant time.

Do what makes you happy, be with those you make you smile and laugh as much as you breathe.

I had an appointment to see a different surgeon, Dr Rhodes, who was in charge of my final surgery. He was a youngish, well-dressed man who was particularly thorough in his examination. He said I'd be a good candidate for his surgery, which is known as a DIEP flap, to removing fat from my lower abdomen and use it to make a new, more natural-feeling breast. He explained it was a complex procedure that involved removing it from one blood supply and reattaching it to another. It would probably take a minimum of eight hours, even if there were no complications. I would be left with a scar just below my knicker line that would stretch from hip to hip. I would not be able to move for a few days, and I would definitely be having my old friends, "the drains" put in place. If I'd been told that twelve months earlier, I would have run for the hills.

This time I was focused on the end result and wanted to start living life to the full again. In fairness, I'd already started that! Dr Rhodes explained that due to the redness of my breast because of the radiotherapy, it would be a minimum of another six months before he considered surgery. I felt deflated; I'd thought it would be done and dusted by July and I would not have it hanging over me.

Julie and I wanted to go to Mohill in County Leitrim to a horse fair in October. It had been a goal for both of us, to celebrate the end of a horrendous year and the start of a new, amazing one. A few of our other friends were eager to come too. This was where my mum and dad were born and raised, and we spent many happy childhood holidays there. The people of Leitrim were always so friendly and welcoming whenever we came over. (Thankfully we did get to go in August 2017 and we had an absolute blast).

The doctor explained that I would need another CT scan of my lower abdomen so that he could see if all my veins were viable.

He was adamant that my oestrogen-inhibiting implants could no longer be injected into my abdomen as he could feel the bruising from the last ones and I had to make sure that my abdomen remained scar and bruise free. I tried to look on the bright side; I would be getting a tummy tuck and a more natural looking breast at the same time. I joked to Liam that I would be cooking the Christmas dinner in a bikini top and hot pants.

I had to have a mammogram of my right breast as it was coming up to a year since it was last checked. When I went into the room, I saw a lady with her partner huddled over with worry, fear etched across their faces. It took me back twelve months to when I was sitting in that position with Liam at the Spire Hospital, and I felt so bloody sorry for her. When her husband left, she told me in a small voice that she'd been rushed there as she'd found a lump. I reassured her as best as I could and explained that I'd been in her position. All treatment was doable.

A few weeks later, I found out that the cancer had not been seen in my other breast. I sincerely hope that the lady in the waiting room had the same news.

My CT scan appointment came through for the QE2. Liam and I made our 9.20 appointment by the skin of our teeth. I dreaded these appointments because they involved putting an IV catheter in, and this was even harder due to the chemo damage on my right arm and hand. I hardly spoke on the journey because I was so scared.

When we arrived, the nurse informed us that the CT scanner was broken, and the scan couldn't go ahead. I burst into tears. On the way home I got a phone call to say that Lister Hospital could do it, so we made our way straight there. Two nurses tried to get a vein but my veins kept blowing once the needle was inserted. I kept my hand firmly clasped around my comforting cross; I was absolutely bawling by then and so distraught.

I was taken back into the room with a doctor with an ultrasound machine to see if she could locate some veins. She failed too, so I was sent home with a sore arm, crying my eyes out and nothing to show for it. They would send another appointment by post. This time, they were going to book an anaesthetist as they felt he or she would be more skilled at locating my elusive veins.

My children were so upset when they heard that the doctors couldn't get a vein for my CT scan. They'd been thinking about it all day at school, relieved that I was going to have another procedure crossed off my list.

The following day, when I picked up Orla from school, she broke down in the car. She told me that it had all became too much for her at school and she had started sobbing. The teacher quickly removed her from the class and spent time with her. God love Orla, she told me that she sobbed for about three-quarters of an hour, explaining how tough our year had been and how gutted she was that I didn't get my CT scan. I suppose it was the straw that broke the camel's back, and she needed some release. It is so hard on all your family members when someone in your tight-knit group becomes ill.

I went back a few weeks later and the anaesthetist successfully located my vein, so my CT scan went ahead. I was over the moon as I wasn't poked and prodded so much.

I was desperate to find out if I carried the faulty BRCA gene and my doctors were appealing for me to be tested. This would help me know if Orla and my three sisters might have an increased risk of developing breast cancer. If I was positive, I'd need to have the other breast removed at the same time as my big operation. I would also have my ovaries removed later because I would have an increased risk of developing ovarian cancer. Honest to God, this cancer stuff is such a minefield.

We'd decided to go to Donegal for a month in the summer. We'd never been for so long before, and we thought we might as well take this opportunity whilst I wasn't working. I had a phone call from my doctor when we were on holiday to say that, despite all her appeals for me to have the BRCA gene test, I'd been refused. She was very annoyed and explained that the NHS needs you to fit into a certain box; if you don't, then that is it. I suppose it all comes down to money.

I decided to get the BRCA gene done privately because it would always worry me, and my appointment with my surgeon was looming closer. The test would take four weeks, so timing was of the essence. It cost £1,500 and included testing for BRCA 1, BRCA 2 and other breast cancer genes which I hadn't heard of. A councillor had to ring me beforehand to go through my family history. It was interesting to hear that, because my dad had no sisters, there was a chance that the mutated breast cancer gene had gone down his line undetected.

The phone call lasted about forty-five minutes. It was agreed that the test (which would be done through my saliva) would be sent to my sister's address in Northern Ireland because it would arrive there sooner than if it was sent to Donegal.

My sister drove it down to me the next day. I followed the instructions and sent it back with my sister so she could post it in Northern Ireland. Now it was a waiting game. To be honest, I didn't think about the results as I would have been driven insane. I made myself forget about it completely for the three weeks that I was in Ireland. I learnt that worrying is like a rocking chair; it will give you something to do but won't get you anywhere.

Just shy of the four-week time frame, when I was back in the UK, I received a call from a withheld number. The lady on the phone explained that they had the results and I would be getting a phone call from a councillor at 7pm that evening to go through them. That scared me; I thought they were preparing me for bad news.

Fiona asked me if this was normal practice and I told her I didn't know. She said maybe I should have asked. I explained that getting information four hours in advance would have driven me demented.

Donna and Joanna called round and, at two minutes to seven, the phone call came. I told the lady on the phone that I was handing two spare phones to my sisters so they could listen too. The councillor said that all my genes had tested normal and there was no greater risk of my daughter or my sisters getting breast cancer, although she did stress that they should still check themselves.

We all shouted out 'Yes!' and I couldn't get the woman off the phone quick enough. I burst into tears when I put down the phone, but for once they were happy tears.

Life is kind of like a party.
You invite a lot of people, some leave early,
some stay all night, some laugh with you and
some show up really late.
But in the end, after the fun, there are
a few who stay to help clean up the mess.
And most of the time, they aren't even
the ones who made the mess.
These people are your true friends.
They are the ones who really matter.

My oncologist made an appointment with a nurse for me to receive four sessions of acupuncture at one-week intervals to try and banish the hot flushes. It may seem odd considering my hatred of needles, but I found that I coped remarkably well. The needles didn't go in deeply and were tiny; I didn't feel some of them at all. The nurse had to make sure she avoided my left arm because of the lack of lymph nodes, and below my belly button as this was the site of my operation. I definitely think that this complementary therapy helped as it appeared to reduce my hot flushes. I was also advised to avoid alcohol, so I had a sober September.

I went back to speak to my surgeon in September because he needed to examine me and discuss the surgery again. He asked me to sit in the waiting room as he had another lady to see. After ten minutes or so, he called me through. He said that the lady in his room was eight weeks post-DIEP surgery and, with her permission, he wanted to show me how she looked.

She told me that she was very happy with the outcome; she'd had a delayed reconstruction and finally she felt like her breast was back. She had an angry scar stretching from hip to hip, but I tried not to focus on that. She said that the two days after the op were horrendous, but after that it was okay. She described the overwhelming fatigue; after she was discharged from the hospital, she couldn't even muster the energy to smile.

A date was made for my surgery on the 25th of October, two months before Christmas. I was very happy with this, as was Liam, because we were thinking of spending Christmas and New Year in Ireland and by then I should be feeling better.

The surgeon explained that most ladies find it takes at least three months before they feel normal again. A lot of them had told him that they were constantly tired and needed lots of naps during the day. We thought Ireland would be good for us as I could rest when I needed to.

At the beginning of October, I found it incredibly hard to sleep at night. I was constantly dreaming about the impending operation and I couldn't get it out of my mind. Three weeks before the operation, I received a phone call from my surgeon's secretary explaining that it would have to put back to 22nd November as another lady needed to take my place. I sobbed my eyes out down the phone; I'd had my head and heart set on the October date.

Liam was adamant that we were not going to go to Ireland; the car and boat journey would be too much and flying wasn't an option due to my blood clot. I told him that, all being well, we would still go and we would focus on that. I found out afterwards that the poor lady who'd taken my place had a cancerous lump removed. My surgery was more cosmetic rather than treatment.

I went to see the pre-op team on the 14th of October to be assessed for the operation. I'd been feeling particularly breathless but hadn't mentioned it to my family as I didn't want to worry them. Mum came with me, and we were told that we would be in and out within the hour.

When the nurse attempted to take my blood, I explained that my veins were awful. She just laughed and said, 'Everyone says that.'

She tried about five times with no luck. I told her about my breathing, so she contacted my surgeon to see what he suggested. She finally managed to get hold of him after two hours. Dr Rhodes told her in no uncertain terms that I needed a CT scan; he would not operate until he knew I wasn't an anaesthetic risk.

Mum was called into the room. I was sobbing because I knew that an intravenous catheter was required and I hated being poked and prodded. Mum started to cry too when she saw how frantic I was.

I was sent down to ambulatory care. The doctor explained that he could see my vein clearly and he would insert a catheter into my arm. He tried at least six times, and the nurse and another doctor tried, but they couldn't get the catheter in. They even sent for an extremely expensive catheter that had never failed them – and that wouldn't go in either.

They wheeled in the ultrasound machine and tried a few times with that. The doctor seemed confident that he'd inserted the catheter but, when he went to flush it, I felt pain in my arm. I explained, but he was adamant that it was in, and he couldn't understand my pain.

I was put in a wheelchair. Mum walked alongside me, visibly worried as I was wheeled by a porter to the CT scanner. Three elderly men were waiting; one must have had a bad fall because, God love him, his face was a mass of blue and purple bruises.

I was finally wheeled into the scanner. The nurse explained the importance of the cannula being in the correct place because the dye would be injected at an unusually high speed and it was vital that it went into my vein. I explained my reservations, so she checked it. She injected saline into the cannula but it came straight back out again. It turned out that the cannula had a kink in it, so that it why it wasn't working properly.

She removed it and tried another three times, but all her attempts were futile. I was sent back outside to my mum and told to go back to ambulatory care and wait for an anaesthetist. I was sobbing again. Boy, did I feel guilty walking past those brave old men crying my eyes out when they were waiting to have their CT scans done.

By then, Mum and I had been waiting ten hours. Mum had refused to leave my side even to get something to eat. At one point, she talked about her friend who'd had cancer; Mum had visited her in hospital about a week before she died. Mum told me that her friend was in great spirits and even talked about going to a wedding which she'd been invited to. 'Then bang, she was dead!'

I told her that these stories were not really helping me. We laughed and Mum apologised; I think we were just stir crazy by then.

We were told that the anaesthetist was in theatre and to come back in half an hour. We went to the hospital café but it was closed, so we bought a sandwich and crisps in the newsagents. Finally, the anaesthetist came and managed to find my vein. I underwent the CT scan and was sent back to the waiting room.

I picked up a magazine and started thumbing through it. An article caught my eye about how to deal with secondary cancer and the questions you may need to ask. I thought this was God's way of telling me gently that the cancer had spread. I showed Mum the article; she'd caught sight of it too but tried to hide the magazine at the bottom of the pile so I wouldn't see it.

Finally, another doctor arrived and stood over us with all my notes in his hand. He told us that my results were clear: there was no evidence of a blood clot or any of the cancer spreading. Mum and I cried and thanked him repeatedly. I threw my arms around Mum and thanked her for staying with me, then rang Liam who was over the moon. We had been in the hospital for twelve hours, but it felt like twelve minutes when we got that news.

I have good friends in County Cork. Two of the girls are sisters, Patsy and Lorraine; I spent a year with them in Australia, travelling and working all down the east coast back in 1999. After that I lived with them in Edinburgh and befriended another Cork girl called Mary. I hadn't seen these girls in years, but they flew over for a couple of days mid-November to see me. Being reunited, having people round me, keeping busy and trying not to think of the operation was just the therapy I needed.

I arranged with five other girlfriends – Helen, Cathy, Claudia, Collette and Katie – to fly to Donegal and have one last hoolie before the op. We had a ball from start to finish. We got to the airport early and Helen managed to get us into the airport lounge where we consumed vast amounts of alcohol. We almost missed our flight as we were having such good craic and got on our plane by the skin of our teeth.

We continued to drink (apart from Collette, who is teetotal) on the plane so we were in fine spirits when my sister Fiona picked us up from Belfast. She told Mum afterwards that we were all so happy and hyper when we got into her car. She dropped us at her home in Dungiven as she had to work that night. We had a car there, so we gave a quick kiss to Fiona's kids and headed off down the road to Donegal.

We had the music on full blast with Zac Brown blowing out the speakers. Collette, God love her, drove like the hammers of hell with us laughing and singing all the way to Gleneely, then we threw our bags into the house and headed over to meet Julie, Louise and Amanda in Carndonagh.

We had a bloody ball that night. We went out the next night too, and it was like having magic medicine. It was a crazy, fun-filled, jam-packed, forty-eight hours in Ireland, definitely not for the faint hearted. For those two days I didn't think much about what lay ahead of me.

My temporary reconstructed breast now felt like a bowling ball; it was solid, hard and deformed due to the radiotherapy. I always knew it was only a temporary procedure, but it was like it had now gone way past its sell-by date.

A smooth sea has never made a skilful sailor.

The day before the surgery, I managed to get Liam and I tickets to see an Irish play in Watford. It was really good and a distraction from anyone coming to visit or having to speak to people. I knew that I was vulnerable and would have broken down if I received any kindness or encouragement.

I got up exceptionally early the day of the procedure as I had to bath in hibiscrub (an antibacterial solution) to minimise the risk of infection – I had bathed in it the night before, too. I also had to drink a special pre-op solution to ensure that I had all sufficient nutrients for the long procedure which lay ahead of me.

Liam and I were fretful as we drove to the hospital. The waiting room was particularly busy, but I was called through straight away. The nurse went through a list of questions and I changed into my stylish hospital gown and matching green socks. The doctor laughed because I had written 'DO NOT USE' in black permanent marker pen on my left arm. I didn't want the nursing team to make a mistake when I was asleep or groggy and inject anything into that arm as I would be at a greater risk of lymphedema. Once you have lymphedema, it remains a problem for life.

When the surgeon came into the room, Liam kissed me and left. There was nothing more he could do. I was wheeled into theatre where, once again, the anaesthetist had a nightmare trying to locate my vein. They ended up going through my wrist and I was crying loads. That's all I remember until I woke up.

My mouth was dry but the nurse could only give me tiny mouthfuls of water. Both of my arms were so tender that it was agony to move them; I assume that was because of the way they'd been positioned for my surgery. The procedure had taken ten hours. It seemed a crazy amount of time, but I was so relieved it was over.

Liam and the kids came to visit, but unfortunately it took so long for the recovery team to allocate a bed that they had to go home without seeing me. I vaguely remember being wheeled into a room of my own and the nurse being told that I had to be kept exceptionally warm. They put something called a 'bear hugger' on me, a plastic blanket filled with warm air.

I had to have checks of my blood pressure, oxygen sats and temperature every hour by the night nurse, and a doctor also visited every hour as well to check my reconstruction. Each time she came in, she seemed concerned about how pale the op site was looking and checked the capillary refill time. This is when they press down on the newly reconstructed breast and monitor the amount of time it takes to bounce back to the colour it should be. The breast was taking longer and longer to return to the right colour.

I didn't realise how alarming this was for the doctor. I kept waking through the night and thanking God aloud that the operation was over. I didn't get into the mind frame that something was badly wrong. I rang Liam and my mum the next morning; they were both so happy that it was over and I was fine.

At one point in the early hours, one of the doctors mentioned putting leeches on me to try and promote blood flow to that area. I mentioned this to Liam in my phone call but he seemed to think that I was still drowsy and hallucinating from the anaesthetic. He rang to check in with me whilst he was walking Dillon and arranged to visit me later.

A short time later, a lady called me to say she was in the park and had found Dillon barking like mad and notably distressed as he couldn't find his owner. She'd seen my number on his collar. I explained that I was in hospital and I would forward Liam's number so that she could ring him. The pain in my arms was excruciating and it took me a long to time to text the phone number.

At about 9am there was a flurry of activity. Suddenly there were about ten of the medical team, including my surgeon, around my bed. They explained that the reconstruction was not receiving the blood supply that it should, and I could end up losing it. That completely threw me. I had to go straight back into theatre; time was of the essence if there was any way they could save it.

I rang Liam to tell him. He was devastated, as was my dad who was with him. I broke down crying and handed the phone to the nurse because I couldn't talk. I asked her to ring my mum and explain as I was not for talking. I was so deflated that I had this complication so soon after a major surgery.

The tea lady on the ward was sweet. She came into my room, held my hand and reassured me that I was going to be okay. I had to sign lots of consent forms, which was laborious due to the pain in both my arms. I was told that if they didn't find the reason for the reconstructed breast not getting the blood supply, the likelihood of losing it would be high. I couldn't believe that all this might have been done in vain.

I was wheeled back into theatre. The anaesthetists decided to use the cannula in my foot – I hadn't even noticed that I had one there – then they placed a mask over my face and gave me an injection to knock me out for the second round of surgery.

I awoke for the second time from my anaesthetic. The procedure had taken four hours; the complication was a twisted blood vessel that had caused lots of clots. It had been a good decision to operate again as I would have lost the reconstruction if they hadn't.

I was relieved that it was all finally over. I kept drifting in and out of sleep; I would feel like I'd been asleep for hours but, bizarrely, when I woke up it had only been about ten minutes each time.

I had an intravenous drip and a morphine pump. Unfortunately, due to my collapsing veins, the morphine pump had to be removed so I no longer had power over my pain relief. I stayed on oral morphine liquid for about three days and then changed to paracetamol. Morphine made me extremely constipated and the pain of going to the toilet far outweighed its pain-killing properties. I was apprehensive about coughing or sneezing; I feared this would rip open my abdominal sutures which stretched from one hip to the other. I felt like a magician's prop because I had literally been sawn almost in half.

My hands, especially my fingers, were swollen and waxy like pork sausages. I begged the nurses to remove my urinary catheter because even thinking about it made me feel queasy and I knew I wouldn't get better until it was gone. I said that I would go to the toilet independently, and I made a significant improvement after that.

The first time I managed to get out of bed and sit in the chair beside it was shattering. The exhaustion hit me like a ton of bricks; I felt like I had climbed a mountain. When I was able to shower and wash my hair, I felt I had conquered the world!

I seemed to go from strength to strength after that, and by Friday I had managed to walk around the ward. I looped arms with Ethan and Orla during visiting and was even showing off doing the moonwalk for them, as well as 'the dab'.

*If the finish line feels too far away,
don't look at it. Just look down at
your feet and take your next, best step*

On the Saturday, I didn't feel good at all. I had severe stomach cramps from the constipation, and I was unusually feverish. In the early hours of Sunday morning, I woke up as I was so hot. I fell back to sleep again, only to wake because I was freezing cold. My nightgown was soaking with sweat.

I pressed the buzzer and the nurse came in. As she changed my gown, we noticed that the reconstruction was now red, swollen and angry looking. The nurse bleeped for an emergency doctor. He put a needle in it, but nothing came out so he assumed that the intravenous antibiotics that I was already on should sort it.

However, the next day one of the doctors expressed concern that I was so swollen. Joanna was with me as he explained that I might need further surgery to find out what was wrong. I cried my eyes out; surely I'd been through enough already.

It was decided that I would have to go to another hospital with a proper breast-scanning machine as they were convinced the reconstruction was filling with fluid and the drain, which was still in, was not doing its job. I couldn't go to the other hospital immediately, however, because the lady who worked the breast scanner was only there on certain days. I was incredibly worried; every time I looked at my reconstruction, it was angrier and redder. I feared it would explode or the stitches would burst because of the pressure behind it.

I was taken to the QE2 Hospital the next day. Sad as it may sound, I was quite excited; I was getting out of the Lister for a day trip. When the porter pushed my wheelchair into the lift and I caught sight of my crazy hair in the mirror, I looked like the nutty professor who'd received an electric shock. I laughed with the porter at the state of it and he reckoned I could start a new trend, though I didn't think it would ever catch on.

I felt quite vulnerable when I arrived at the QE2 because I was still in my hospital robe in a wheelchair, whilst all the other women were in their own clothes waiting for their appointments.

Eventually I was called through and examined carefully with the breast scanner. The doctor was extremely gentle as she sensed my pain. She concluded that there was no fluid in the breast, just lots of swelling. I felt a bit gutted as I was taken back to the Lister Hospital. One of the nurses explained that this was probably a better outcome; if there was fluid, they might have needed to operate again to find out where it was coming from. I changed onto a stronger course of antibiotics.

My surgeon came in my room about 10.30pm a week later. He explained that he had performed the same operation on another lady that day, but he just couldn't get me out of his mind. He apologised, and said it was very rare that this operation went so terribly wrong. When he'd first met me, he was convinced that I would be home three to five days after surgery. He seemed so humble and I felt quite sorry for him; I was obviously a massive dent to his surgical expertise and his unblemished surgical record.

Liam kept saying that Ireland was out of the question for Christmas as I wouldn't be fit for it. I told him to hold his horses; we'd see how I was. Mum kept trying to pump me with homemade soups and fresh fruit to build me up.

I felt so sad when I saw the nurses decorating the hospital for Christmas. A friend sent me a link to the song 'Fairy Tale of New York' and I sang along with it in my side room with the tears rolling down my cheeks. It's my favourite Christmas song. However, that time, sitting alone in my bed, it was bittersweet and I longed to be home.

The nurses were so good and I think they were also upset that my hospital stay was so long. It was quite funny one night when the nurse was changing the dressing on my abdomen. I looked down and noticed that my old belly button was gone and I had a brand new one in its place! No one had told me that was going to happen, so it was a bit of a shock!

I finally got out of hospital after two long weeks. I was so happy to be finally leaving, overcome with emotion. While Liam and I were waiting for the lift to take us to the car, along with about twenty other people, Fiona sent a video of her two children welcoming me home. The floodgates opened there and then, and I started to sob. Liam was standing open-mouthed, saying, 'What's wrong now?' I think he could have killed Fiona.

Of course, we got to Ireland. That was always going to happen. I made sure I kept my surgical stockings on and packed all my dressings, as I had to redress my reconstruction daily. My surgeon, although not overly happy about me leaving the country, gave me some antibiotics to use if I thought there was another infection. The long trip to Cairnryan in Scotland to catch the boat was fine; I slept in the back seat and got out a couple of times to stretch my legs. I picked up our spare car from Fiona in Dungiven and drove it back; that way I got to spend an hour with Fiona and her kids, too.

We had a great Christmas and New Year in the Emerald Isle. The kids were particularly spoilt as the year before hadn't been a great one. Orla got a laptop and Ethan got a quad bike, so they were always out in the fields with that. I felt great; apart from daily dressings, you would never have thought I'd had anything done. However, a few days before New Year's Eve, I noticed a slight odour coming from the op site. This worried me a bit and I feared I might be getting another infection. I started my backup antibiotics and made a mental note to contact my surgery when I got back to the UK.

Keep your face towards the sunshine
and shadows will fall behind you.

Back in Luton, I made an appointment and went to see my surgeon. He didn't seem too concerned and said it was something called 'fat necrosis'. This happens when the fat 'doesn't take' and it dies and becomes necrotic. The body usually absorbs it but, in my case, as I had two holes in the reconstruction the fat could leak out.

I had to attend weekly clinics to check if the holes were closing and have the breast re-dressed for two months, with the odour from the bandages getting progressively worse. The amount of necrotic fat draining from the wound was increasing daily, and I noticed that another hole had opened due to the pressure and yellow fluid was seeping out of it. I was paranoid about being out in public as I needed huge dressings, and the smell was unusually bad. It was vile – it reminded me of a baby's nappy.

I started to feel quite unwell and thought I was coming down with a bout of flu. I explained to the nurses at the Friday dressing clinic how much fluid was coming out; I'd had to get up several times at night to change the dressings. The nurses gave me more absorbent dressings, but the smell was getting worse daily. At night time, I struggled to get warm; my feet were always cold to the point that I started wearing socks to bed.

On the Sunday, I had a bath. I felt cold, shivery and lethargic and was ready to crawl back into bed to try and warm up. I remembered Julie's mum, Rose, who had sadly passed as she didn't get treatment when she started to feel flu-like, and I decided to get dressed and drive to the hospital. I rang Liam and told him that I was en route to the Lister as I really didn't feel that great. I checked myself into the hospital, convinced I'd be sent home with a few antibiotics and all would be fine.

After a long wait, I was called through to see a nurse in the triage room. As soon as she took my vitals, she became visibly alarmed. My temperature was high and my heart rate was elevated. A doctor came through and, with the aid of an ultrasound machine, took some blood and placed a cannula into my vein. A sepsis nurse came into the room and explained that I would need to go on intravenous fluids immediately and start IV antibiotics as I almost certainly had sepsis. She was taken aback at the amount of yellow fluid that was draining from my wound. Another doctor came into the room and said I would not be allowed to eat anything because he thought that I would need emergency surgery in the morning to open the wound and flush it.

I was given huge dressings like nappies to try and absorb the stinking fluid. I'd contacted Liam again and also my mum. There were no beds on the ward for hours, so I was put in a side room and left there for ages with my drip. Joanna came in to see me, as well as Fiona who had flown over the night before. I was extremely tearful, so frustrated by the smell and the amount of fluid that was coming from my chest.

I was finally allocated a bed about four hours later but I couldn't warm up and I was shaking with the cold. The male nurse kept giving me more blankets – in the end, I was lying on the bed with seven of them.

The ward housed four women. A homeless lady was in the bed opposite me and the other two ladies really looked down their noses at her. Whenever she went out for a smoke, they badmouthed her, saying that she was stealing from the canteen and the shop downstairs because she always came back with a bag full of 'goodies'. I didn't get involved; it was none of my business and nobody knew that woman's circumstances.

The following morning, my surgeon came to see me. He was so disappointed that I was back in hospital but made it clear that I was not to undergo emergency surgery because this would be a huge risk to the reconstruction and I could lose it. He was happy for me to continue on the strong intravenous antibiotics and explained that I needed to massage the area well when I was in the shower to try and get as much drained from my body.

I told him that I didn't have any shower gel because I'd not known that I was going to be admitted. When the curtain was pulled back, the homeless lady very kindly handed me her unopened shampoo, conditioner and shower gel. She'd obviously overheard the conversation. This simple gesture was overwhelming; this poor lady had nothing to her name but shared what she had. God love her, she offered me her comb too, though I declined that as I don't think she'd ever washed her own hair, despite all her cleaning products.

Luckily, Liam arrived later with Ethan and Orla. Orla had packed me a bag with my washing essentials and bought me bed socks to try and keep me warm. I was gutted as it was my birthday that day – Valentine's Day – and there I was, stuck in a hospital bed. The nurses tried different bandages to absorb the fluid but nothing worked. I woke up every few hours in the night soaked through, and the odour was nauseating. Every night involved the laborious task of changing the bandages, my nightgown and the sheets. In the end, they brought a stoma nurse in and she attached two paediatric stoma bags to the open holes on the reconstruction. It was unbelievable – there was now no smell from the wound and I didn't have to keep changing the bandages in the night. Finally, I could sleep through without waking up; all I had to do was empty the stoma bags once they were full. They did stink when I emptied them, but it was a million times better than before.

I was getting quite anxious in the hospital as we were planning a weekend away with all my family in a big house in the country. It had been booked for ages to celebrate Fiona's fortieth, Kieran's thirtieth and Mum's seventieth birthdays. Liam kept saying there was no way that I could go now. I didn't say anything but then Mum joined in too, saying that it was no big deal that I couldn't go. However, unknown to both of them, I'd told the doctors that I needed to be out by Friday morning, and I would go on oral antibiotics or inject myself through the IV line. The doctor was not happy and told me it would not be advisable because oral antibiotics were not as good as intravenous ones, and the hospital would not let me leave with an intravenous catheter.

I was so feckin frustrated that day. I cried my eyes out and told him that I was sick to death of hospitals, I wished that I'd never had the surgery done (that was the only time I ever made that comment) and I was going on my weekend away, come hell or high water!

By the Friday morning, I'd packed my bag, showered and changed out of my hospital gown. I then paced the corridors looking for the doctor as I couldn't go until I had my antibiotics. I was like a cat on a hot tin roof. The nurses, the cleaner and the tea lady were all rooting for me; they knew how much this weekend meant.

I spotted my surgeon coming out of a meeting with his team and I legged it back to my bed – which had my suitcase sitting on it.

When he came to me, he looked at me. I smiled and asked politely, 'Please could I have my prescription?' I think we both knew that I was leaving the hospital to go on my break.

Fiona picked me up and I went straight to the hairdressers for a wash and blow dry. I got home, packed mine and the kid's cases and drove to Peterborough to our weekend away. We were the first ones to arrive. It was a brilliant fun-filled weekend, and I am so glad I was there. I'd have been gutted if I'd missed out. My way of thinking was that I'd had five days of intravenous antibiotics, and now could top up with the oral antibiotics.

Embrace uncertainty.
Some of the most beautiful chapters
in our lives won't have a
title until much later

About 5 weeks later, I ended up back in hospital for eleven hours when I started to get sepsis symptoms again. This time I was much luckier and, after a long wait, was given oral antibiotics. The effect of the fat necrosis had a massive impact on my reconstruction. My surgeon was visibly shocked at how it decreased in size, so much so that I had to start wearing a prosthesis, which felt heavy and awkward. I also had a knitted prosthesis made by a charity called Knitted Knockers – how remarkable is that? You let them know your cup size and what colour you'd like, and they knit you one (or two, if needed).

I had been stuffing socks in my bra on nights out so that I didn't look lopsided. I asked the surgeon if he could put an implant in there instead, but he refused. He was adamant that my body would reject it.

Radiation had a massive, detrimental impact on my body. Although I looked fine on the outside, the veins in my chest area were irreversibly damaged. Dr Rhodes said that I would need least four more surgeries to try and rebuild the failed reconstruction, each involving a general anaesthetic and removing fat from another area, such as my abdomen or thighs, and injecting it into the breast area. My body would hopefully accept this better as it was my own fat. I would be seen as a day patient and be able to go home that night. This way, I would not be taking up a much-needed NHS bed. The reason for so many surgeries was the risk of fat reabsorption into the body, which can be quite high.

We wouldn't know how successful each operation would be until three months afterwards, when any fat would have died or been reabsorbed, so each surgery would be done at three-month intervals. This is known as lipo modelling. I burst into tears when the surgeon told me; I thought enough is enough, I am so nearly there but I still haven't reached the finishing line. The surgeon apologised again but 'promised to get me right'.

My mum rang when I was leaving the hospital and I burst into tears. Joanna rang me back and I was so deflated.

The next day, when I had slept on it, I realised that this was the best option for me. At the end of the day it was a cosmetic procedure, not a cancer treatment. There were people out there getting horrendous news in the doctor's consulting room, and I really needed to pull myself together.

It was a long drawn-out process and I ended up having many more surgeries than first anticipated. Each time I had to be gassed down as the anaesthetist always struggled to locate my veins. My abdomen would be covered in large purple painful bruises post op. Thankfully I am a quick healer. A few months after each procedure some of the fat had been absorbed back into my body and therefore more operations were required by the surgeon to obtain good symmetry.

After more surgeries, my surgeon sat me down and informed me the only option was to reduce the other breast. He was never going to be able to match it because my body had reacted so badly to the radiotherapy. Liam was understandably reluctant, worried that if anything went wrong I would be affected on both sides.

I did think long and hard about it but decided to go with it. It was hard looking into a mirror and I started to avoid it. I wanted normality again.

Life is like the ocean.
It can be calm or still, and rough or rigid,
but in the end, it is always beautiful.

When I woke up from my breast reduction, I was dumbfounded. I initially thought that my surgeon had performed a mastectomy on the other side because my chest was completely taped up. I knew I couldn't talk to Liam about my concerns as he was the one who'd asked me not to do it. I didn't want to hear him say, 'I told you so.'

When I went to the post-op dressing clinic and they removed the bandages, I was pleased to see that I did look more symmetrical through all the bruising. I found out that my surgeon had removed 525g of breast tissue, which is quite a significant amount.

I had regular check-ups with the breast-care team, including mammograms and bone scans. The bone scans are called DEXA scans and are painless. They are used to measure the density of bone mass. I found out that I had osteopenia – bone thinning – a step down from osteoporosis. This was a side effect brought on by my chemo, radiotherapy, and medication. I had to now add vitamin D and calcium to my daily medication.

In May 2020, I found another hard lump further up on my chest wall. I rang the hospital and they made an emergency appointment for the next day. Miss Darcy, my lovely lady surgeon, felt it and stated she wanted it scanned immediately. That really did freak me out, and I was sure the cancer was back.

I had told no one but Liam. As I sat in the chair waiting to be seen by the sonography team, I decided that I would not tell anyone until after the bank holiday weekend. I was petrified that I was getting on this feckin roller coaster again, and convinced that my bones were thinning because my body was riddled in cancer.

The sonographer and a nurse laid me down on a bed and took lots of images, then I was asked to sit back in the waiting room. When I was called back to the consulting room, Miss Darcy informed me that it was just some necrotic fat which had migrated up the chest wall; she would give me antibiotics. She hugged me and said she was glad I was doing so well. I can tell you that was some relief – I was so elated I could have jumped through the roof of the hospital.

More fat-transfer operations followed. Post op, I had to keep my waist, from where they took the fat, tightly bound to stop swelling or fat migrating back into those channels where the probes had been placed during surgery. I bought a great contraption on Amazon which was like a waist trainer with Velcro tightening straps. That was all well and good, until I was halted at the airport when we were going to Ireland on holiday. I was stopped and searched by the female security guard, then ushered into a side room and asked to remove it so they could see I wasn't hiding drugs or guns. It was highly embarrassing, but I understood they were just doing their job.

'Which is more important,' asked Big Panda,
'the journey or the destination?'
'The company,' said Tiny Dragon

My final operation, my fourteenth surgery, was performed in a private hospital in Hatfield in August 2020. If anyone had told me that I would have to undergo so many, I would have run for the hills.

The hospital was state of the art – I was blown away. I had a room to myself with an en-suite; even my surgical socks were a bright white instead of the usual green. My usual surgeon did the procedure, but the reason that I had my operation in a private hospital was because of the COVID pandemic which started that year. NHS hospitals were no longer able to perform routine procedures.

When I came round from the surgery, I was given a menu and I could pick anything I wanted for my lunch. The surgeon wanted to see me after the operation, so I had to wait until he was ready, and the chef came into my room asking me to choose my dinner! I was quite gutted when Liam came to collect me.

My post-op check six weeks later revealed that my surgeon was finally satisfied with the outcome, and I was too. I had come to the end of a long road for operations and procedures, and that felt incredible. I was finally free.

Cancer has changed me so much as a person. I live more for the moment now than ever before. I am up for everything and love spontaneity. I travel more. I am more in touch with nature and love to see the changes as each season ends and another one begins. It's therapeutic to smell the flowers and 'drink in' your surroundings. I don't ever want to be buried with 'what ifs?' and 'why didn't I do that?'. I would urge people to regularly check their body for any abnormalities as cancer doesn't always manifest itself as a palpable lump. Any delays or hesitations can mean huge changes to your treatment plan, and ultimately, your diagnosis.

I cry a lot more than I ever did. If I see someone with a bald head obviously from cancer, that can trigger it. I remember one day after about my eighth surgery the surgeon showed me my various stages (photos are taken before each procedure) and I cried because of how I used to look before the cancer. We often have unreal expectations about how we should look. When I saw those photos, I realised how hard I'd been on myself when I'd actually looked just fine. I cannot put into words how amazing our NHS has been – the surgeons, nurses, receptionists, cleaners, and never forgetting the tea ladies/men and volunteers. These are all the very fibres that are woven into the cloth of our fantastic health system.

I am finally happy with how my body looks, but it has taken a long time. I hated looking in the mirror, but now I'm proud of my scars because I've earned them. I'm still standing and I'm still here.

There is an element of survivor's guilt too. Many people who were diagnosed long after me are no longer here: good, honest, lovely people who have passed. That upsets me a lot. They fought just as hard as me, if not harder, but sometimes it comes down to the cards we are dealt with in life.

I want to end this book on a happy note by saying thank you to everyone for everything – the late-night phone calls, the early morning texts, the walks, the car drives, the thoughtful gifts, the food and making me feel so very loved. Cancer is ugly, but what comes out of having it is something beautiful and heart-warming. There are so many kind-hearted and wonderful people out there.

As I finish writing this book, we are still in lockdown because of the COVID pandemic. I can assure you that, once restrictions are lifted and the world slowly goes back to normal, I'll be back enjoying life to the full and not wasting one minute of it. I will be the one in the departure lounge with a cocktail in one hand and a meal deal in the other. Simple things are often the best.

Slainte x

Printed in Great Britain
by Amazon

16694048R00081